THE MIDDLE-CLASS MILLIONAIRE

AN EASY-TO-FOLLOW BLUEPRINT TO SAVE, INVEST, AND ACHIEVE FINANCIAL FREEDOM

JAMES SPAULDING

The Middle-Class Millionaire:
An Easy-to-Follow Blueprint to Save, Invest and Achieve
Financial Freedom
Published by Chambray Lane Publishing
Charlotte, NC

ISBN: 979-8-218-56284-7

Finance / Wealth Management

Cover and interior design by Asya Blue Design, copyright owned by James Spaulding.

CHAMBRAY LANE

PUBLISHING

CONTENTS

Disclaimer

Everything in this book is simply my opinion, based on what has worked for me. It may not continue to work for me, and it might not work for you.

I hope this book provides you with ideas and guidance on how to think smarter about your financial decisions; however, I certainly don't know the facts and circumstances unique to any reader's personal situation.

As the author, I make no certification or representation as to accuracy, completeness, currentness, suitability, or validity of any information in this book and will not be liable for any errors, omissions, losses, injuries, or damages arising from this book. All information is provided on an as-is basis.

You are solely responsible for your own choices. There are absolutely no guarantees explicitly relayed or implied.

Introduction

HOW TO INTERACT WITH THIS BOOK

This is something of an unusual book; it's part textbook, part workbook, and part reference guide.

The questionnaire at the beginning of chapter 1 is the initial screening form I use in my personal finance coaching business. It's designed to identify clients I believe I can help. I can't be all things to all people, so, I decided to identify those folks I'm best suited to help.

Along with the questionnaire, I developed my top 20 wealth-building rules to live by. You might not agree with my 20 rules. Agreement is not required. However, these 20 rules have served me well and are a principal reason I'm where I am today. My hope is that these 20 rules will help you in your financial journey as well.

This book is aimed at do-it-yourself folks (DIYers). DIYers are those of us who are willing to change (i.e., improve) their behavior. No one likes change, except for a wet baby, and he cries about it.

If you're looking for a financial planner to handle things for you—in other words, an assets under management (AUM) arrangement—then the internet is full of professionals who can accommodate your desire. AUM planners are the norm, but beware they charge healthy **management fees** for this hands-off approach. Many AUM planners are good at what they do, but most get 1% of your **assets** as their fee annually; whether your assets go up or down, they get paid! Most AUM planners also won't accept you as a client until you have at least $500,000 or $1 million dollars they can manage. My portfolio meets their requirement, but I'm not about to sign over my **assets** to them and their high fees. I'd rather do it myself.

A 2023 J. D. Power (research firm) survey found that only 11% of financial advisors offered comprehensive advice. Many financial advisors are really salespeople, sometimes only selling one product (e.g., whole life insurance). Everything's a nail if you're a hammer. No one will care more about your finances than you! Get educated about personal finance and take control of your future. Don't let money problems short-circuit your relationships and your life goals. I suggest you find a financial coach to work with to help validate that you're on the right path. A good financial coach can help you achieve your goals and think smarter about money.

> **financial coach** – provides personal finance advice, guidance, education, and feedback for do-it-yourself investors, and is compensated by clients on an hourly or fixed fee. A financial coach has the heart of a teacher. A financial coach does *not* actively manage investments or determine financial decisions for you. They mentor and provide consulting style advice only.

There are many things in life way more important than money. But if you ignore the financial aspect of your daily decisions, then negative money consequences will find you, and it won't just affect you, it will affect those closest to you. Don't let the "debt star" destroy you!

If you're ignorant and apathetic about your money decisions, then it's likely your children and family will have to take care of you when you're physically unable to work. For some, this is their early sixties, as 40% are forced to retire earlier than they planned. It's irresponsible to be a burden on others, especially when there's something you can do about it. Let's do something about it *right now*!

One of the most rewarding things you can do with money is to give it away: to those in need, to charitable organizations, or to your family.

You won't be able to give much to any of these worthy causes if you continue to struggle with money.

One of the positive aspects of this book is that you don't need to read it front-to-back like a traditional book. There are chapters that are foundational (e.g., budgeting 101 in chapter 2) that you might have grasped many years ago that can just be skimmed. But carefully read and evaluate the questions (i.e., "homework") after each chapter. Pay special attention to words in bold. These are defined in the glossary at the end of the book.

Each chapter has at least one assignment for you to do with your finances. Don't skip this part! It's where the magic happens. Apply these money lessons to your situation. Ignoring the homework would be like going to the grocery store just to look around. Food is meant for nourishment, not to casually be looked at and dismissed.

When you reach your sixties and seventies, what advice would you want to give your younger self? Don't look back on a life full of regrets or missed opportunities.

I hope this book helps you avoid those financial missteps. I want you to be the best version of yourself possible. You can't achieve that if you don't have a plan. Nobody accidentally qualifies for the Olympics. It takes being intentional and proactive. It means deferring gratitude today (save up for that vacation, don't put it on a credit card!) so you can have a great, big, beautiful tomorrow.

I'm convinced you can succeed with money and achieve your financial freedom. I'm sure of it. If I can do it, most anyone can, because I made many mistakes along the way. But you'll need perseverance to keep on keeping on. Chapter 26 is dedicated to inspirational quotes to keep you motivated along the way on your journey.

Personal finance is a marathon—it's a life journey. This book will help you think smarter about your everyday financial decisions. Years from now, you'll look back and thank your younger self for getting educated and staying committed to achieving financial freedom.

You've got this!

SECTION I

FOUNDATIONS

Chapter 1

WHERE DO YOU START?

Where should you start? At the beginning, of course! Seriously, how should you get started on your personal finance journey? How do you cut through the cacophony of personal finance information (and misinformation) nowadays? I know I wanted **financial stability**, and eventually financial freedom. But what should you do when life happens and you find yourself on a path to financial desolation—full of **credit card** bills, persistent bill collectors, and more month than paycheck.

Sixty percent of Americans (per Bankrate.com) don't have $1,000 saved up for an emergency. Life moves pretty fast (American philosopher Ferris Bueller). You won't have a plumbing problem; you'll have a plumbing emergency.

Sixty percent of Americans don't have a **retirement account**. Fifty percent of millennials (born 1981–1996), and 92% of Gen Z (born 1997–2012), don't have anything saved for **retirement**. **Social security** only replaces 40% of your pre-retirement income, on average. That's only $1,560 per month, which is tough to live on. The **median 401(k)** balance is only $35,000. $35,000 won't take you very far in retirement. Seventy-eight percent of Americans **live paycheck to paycheck**. All these stats make me want to save, save, save.

They don't often teach personal finance in public schools, and many parents don't teach it at home. Many struggle with their finances. But it doesn't have to be that way. Let's come up with a plan, a road map for you to more than just "get by."

"Listen son, a fool with a plan can beat a genius with no plan. Your mother and I are concerned that we have a fool with no plan." (T. Boone Pickens's father).

Let's start with where you are currently, 'cause you can't get where you're going if you don't first know where you are.

Jimmy's Money Tips intake questionnaire from my personal financial coaching business

1. Do you want to retire
   a. At 65
   b. Before 65
   c. After 65
   d. Not planning to retire (I'm not a quitter)

2. Are you committed to becoming financially independent, including a willingness to change your behavior (**deferred gratification, saving, investing,** etc.) to achieve financial independence (FI)?

3. Are you committed to becoming totally debt-free, including a willingness to change your behavior (deferred gratification, **forced scarcity,** etc.), to achieve freedom from debt?

4. Do you track your monthly **expenses**?

5. Do you have a monthly **budget**? A plan to tell your money where to go rather than wondering where it all went?

6. My **net worth** is
    a. Negative (e.g., student loans)
    b. 0$–$99k
    c. $100–$499k
    d. $500–$999k
    e. Greater than $1 million
    f. Not sure

7. Do you have **credit card debt**?
    a. 0$–$4k
    b. $5k–$9k
    c. $10k–$15k
    d. Greater than $15k

8. Do you have a car loan? If so, what is the remaining balance and interest rate?

9. Do you have an **emergency fund**?
    a. 0$–$1,000
    b. 1–3 months living expenses
    c. 4–6 months living expenses
    d. Greater than 6 months living expenses
    e. Not sure what my expenses are

10. Do you currently contribute to retirement accounts?
    a. 0%–5%
    b. 6%–9%
    c. 10%–15%
    d. 16%–20%
    e. Greater than 20%

11. Do you have any financial goals? Briefly list.

12. What do you want to learn and/or accomplish with a **financial coach**? Briefly describe.

13. Do you own or rent your home?

14. What is one thing you would start doing to become financially independent? What is one thing you would stop doing?

I'll demonstrate by taking my own questionnaire. Here goes. . .

1. B, I hope to retire (kinda-sorta-maybe) by 55. I want to be Financially Independent, Recreationally Employed at 55 (some call this Barista FIRE), meaning I'll quit my 9-to-5 corporate job and work on my terms. I'm hoping to become a personal finance coach part-time. Let me define what financially independent means to me. I want to be totally debt-free (including the mortgage) and have roughly 25 times my expenses saved for retirement. By expenses, I mean those that are not covered by Social Security. I don't want to retire from something as much as I want to retire to something—something I'm passionate about. I want freedom from the chains of debt and the daily corporate grind.

2. Yes, I'm committed to becoming financially independent. We've been saving 20% of my salary (including company contributions) for the past twenty-five years. That has meant forced scarcity, living on less than we make, and saving and investing for the future.

3. Yes, I have a plan to be totally debt-free by 55. This will include selling our rental house at some point in the next few years.

4. Yes, I've been tracking my monthly expenses via the EveryDollar app for the past ten years.

5. Yes, I have a monthly budget. However, we might be over in one category while under in another. We're trying to stay on budget each

month, and mostly succeeding, with a few fails along the way . . .

6. E, My net worth is greater than $1 million. I initially breached the 7-figure mark when I was 48, but the **stock market** returns in 2022 knocked me back. I regained the mark a year later and am hoping to stay above and grow from here.

7. A, No, I do not have credit card debt. Having recently turned 50, I'm happy to say we don't have any **credit card debt**; however, we've carried balances before. We had an uncomfortable **credit card** balance right after we started our cabin rental business, and a few other times when we had unexpected **expenses**. I'm the poster child for having a bigger emergency fund—life moves pretty fast!

8. No, I do not have a car loan. I haven't had car payments for several years now. I'm allergic to car payments. I think this is key to being able to spend less than you make. The average monthly car payment (per Experian) is $729 for a new car and $528 for a used car—yikes!

9. Yes, I have an emergency fund, in three layers: (1) We currently have $2,000 in our **credit union** savings account. This helps to buffer the timing of **cash flow** throughout the month (linked to our checking account) since I only get paid once at the end of each month. (2) We have about $9,000 in a brokerage **money market fund** (which can easily be transferred to our checking account in a day or two). (3) This layer, which will be controversial to some, is our **Roth** contributions. We've contributed $18,000 to our Roth accounts over the past five years. You can always access your Roth contributions penalty-free— even before retirement. I don't plan to access these accounts until retirement, but it's the break glass in case of emergency option. Our **basic living expenses** are about $5,000 per month, meaning we have about 5.5 months of expenses we could cover in an emergency without incurring additional debt.

10. E, Yes, I currently contribute 27% to our retirement accounts, including company contributions. I averaged 20% over the first twenty-five years of my career, starting out small around age 25 at about 10%, and ramped up to about 30% in my late forties.

11. My five-year financial goals are to be totally debt-free (including the mortgage); save 25 times annual expenses for retirement (i.e., financial freedom/independence); retire from my corporate job; start a personal finance coaching job part-time; and save three-years' worth of expenses in a **"bridge account,"** which will fund expenses from age 56 to 59.5.

12. I worked with a financial coach shortly before I wrote this book. My goal was to see if I was on the right track on my personal finance journey. I wanted to know what changes I should make to be smarter about my financial decisions, and if I could FIRE by 55.

13. I own my home, which is something of a misnomer. Technically, the bank owns my home but their customer service is excellent. If I miss a payment (I haven't but work with me), they'll call me—several times if need be. They'll even send someone out to sell my home for me if they don't hear back. Talk about customer service . . .

14. I'll pick three things we've changed recently to seek our financial independence. We stopped ordering sodas at restaurants; instead, we order water. We started sharing meals at more expensive restaurants occasionally. And we decided not to pay for any TV service for six months out of the year, utilizing over-the-air broadcasts (free via antenna) and other free on-demand options. We still pay for a streaming service during baseball season. Go Braves! I mean, I have to watch all 162 games, right?!

Jimmy's Top 20 Wealth-Building Rules

1. <u>Live on less than you make.</u> This is foundational. None of my other financial advice works until you get this one right. It's not how much money you make, it's how much you keep! The janitor that saves 20% of his income is better off than the doctor that racks up credit card debt living a luxurious lifestyle. Living **frugally** goes a long way toward achieving this goal, but it doesn't hurt to have an average to above average income as well.

2. <u>Know your why.</u> Why do you want to be financially independent? You'll need to know your motivation because hard times, they are a comin', and you'll give up if you don't think the sacrifice is worth it. Is the juice worth the squeeze? Only you can answer this deeply philosophical question. Do you want financial freedom to pursue a passion project? Mission work? World travel? What are your five- and ten-year goals? Dream big. Write your dreams down, making them real, and let's turn them into a plan.

3. <u>Save early and often.</u> Compound interest and time are on your side if you start saving in your early twenties. Albert Einstein said **compounding** is the 8th Wonder of the World. For example, $1 invested at age 20 could become $77 by age 65. That same $1 will only become $30 by age 65 if you wait to invest until age 30, using 10% returns. "Do it right, do it light, do it wrong, do it long." (Mr. Bo Hanson of *The Money Guy Show* fame). If you do it wrong you'll be working into your seventies. If you start investing just $100 per month at age 20, it could grow to $953,000 by age 65 (investing $54,000 in total). If you wait till age 50 and invest $800 per month (**investing** $144,000 in total), you'll only have $337,000 at age 65, despite having invested almost three times as much as your 20-year-old self (using 9% returns).

I recommend you save 20% of your salary (including company contributions). This might be aspirational in your twenties, but you can start with 5% if that's all you can do and work your way up to 20% (and beyond). Keep it simple—invest in a low-cost **S&P 500 index**. As you get closer to retirement, revisit your asset allocation and consider adding **diversification** (e.g., **bonds**).

4. <u>Avoid debt.</u> Especially consumer/credit card debt. The Bible says the borrower is servant to the lender. I believe there are times when debt is unavoidable, especially for purchasing a home and reliable transportation; but debt, like a chainsaw, should make you nervous. If it doesn't make you nervous, you're doing it wrong. Pay off your debts sooner rather than later. It's a key component on the path to becoming financially independent.

5. <u>Keep an emergency fund.</u> Be prepared. Even a $1,000 starter emergency fund helps buffer you from those unexpected expenses that are surely coming. If you don't have an emergency fund, then you will likely use credit cards or pay bills late and start the spiral toward **payday lender**s and stress-filled kitchen table discussions that might end in divorce. Start with $1,000 but work up to 3–6 months' worth of expenses, saved in a **high-yield savings account**.

6. <u>Get the company match.</u> If you are eligible to participate in a company **401(k)**, it's highly likely the company will match a portion (e.g., 50% up to 6%) of your contributions. This is free money! Don't walk across the street to avoid someone who's trying to hand you money. Don't leave money on the table. Contribute at least enough to get this free money—it comes with a 100% guaranteed **rate-of-return**! 34% of Americans do not contribute enough to get the full **company match**.

7. <u>Budget, budget, budget.</u> I said it three times because it's really important. A budget isn't a straitjacket—it's telling your money where to

go instead of wondering where it went. A budget is the map on your journey to financial freedom. There are many ways to use technology to automate this "chore." I use the EveryDollar app, but there are many other budgeting apps to choose from. Either way, this is a vital step to know where you are so you can slowly build **wealth** on your way to financial freedom.

8. <u>Know your net worth.</u> Add up everything you own, subtract everything you owe, and the result is your net worth. Do you own more than you owe? Do this calculation at least once a year. Set goals to increase your net worth over time. That which is measured tends to improve. If you want to know how much your net worth "should be," multiply your age times your income then divide by 10. For example, if you're 50 and make $100,000 annually, then your net worth should be 50 X $100,000 divided by 10 = $500,000 (*The Millionaire Next Door* formula).

9. <u>Automate your saving/investing.</u> This is a complement to #3 (Save early and often.) Set up your saving and investing to come out of your paycheck each month—*before* you see it! This forces you to adjust your lifestyle to live on less than you earn. Make good habits easy (automated) and bad habits (overconsuming) hard. Regular, consistent investing over time is the best way to achieve financial freedom, eventually. Slow and steady wins the race. Once you adjust your lifestyle to match your take-home pay, you won't miss these contributions. Over time, this saving and investing will grow because of your monthly contributions and the power of compounding. Once given time to do its "magic," eventually **Mr. Market** will be contributing more than you do.

10. <u>Take risks.</u> Following are four risks I've taken in my journey: (1) Obtained a college degree—it's risky because it could cost over $100,000 over four years, and there is no guarantee you'll get a

THE MIDDLE-CLASS MILLIONAIRE

degree or a good job. Seventy-three percent of college graduates don't work in their field of study. I earned my master of accounting degree and credit that with getting a good-paying job. For me, the risk was worth it. (2) Invested in the stock market. Over the past 100 years, the stock market has averaged a 10.5% rate-of-return, but it's not a guarantee. Some years the stock market is up, some years it's down. You have to be disciplined and stay invested, and give your investments time to grow. Compounding can only add its magic if you sprinkle in time. (3) Invested in real estate. We have a cabin we rent out. Real estate can be another great investment, but there are risks. Real estate can go down in value. Renters can damage your property or might not pay the rent on time (or at all). (4) Started a business. Many **millionaires** started their own businesses, but 70% of businesses fail in the first ten years. It's a lot of time and work with a high potential for failure. We started a cabin rental business and it's been a big addition to our **retirement portfolio**. In a couple of years, we'll have a fully paid-for house—that others paid for—that we can sell to become totally debt-free, enabling us to retire early.

11. <u>Start with the end in mind.</u> If **financial independence** is your goal, calculate 25 times your retirement expenses (those not covered by Social Security). Let's do an example. Say you spend $100,000 annually per year pre-retirement. Let's take 80% of $100,000 as an estimate of post-retirement expenses to get $80,000 of annual retirement expenses. We'll estimate your Social Security income at $40,000 (assuming both spouses qualify), which means you need your investments to fund the other $40,000 of annual living expenses in retirement. $40,000 times 25 = $1 million dollars. This is the amount you need to save by age 65. How much do you need to save per month to get to $1 million dollars?

I explained earlier that saving $100 per month from age 20 to age 65 would yield $953,000. Starting with the end in mind also means saving up for your next big purchase, having **sinking funds** for inevitable future expenses. If you own a home, eventually you'll need to replace the roof. Say a new roof costs $20,000 and you estimate you'll need one ten years from now. This means you should set aside $167 per month into a sinking fund, saved in a money market fund and earning 5% interest, while you hurry up and wait for the roof to leak.

12. Buy a house you can easily afford. Rule of thumb is 2.5 times your household income, or no more than 25%–30% of your salary going toward your housing expense. If those numbers seem unreasonable, you might need to get a roommate. Or buy a duplex and rent out half the unit.

13. Buy a car you can pay off in three years. 20/3/8. 20% down, financed for no more than three years, payment no more than 8% of your salary.

14. Choose your spouse wisely. You and your spouse are on the same team. Hopefully rowing the boat in the same direction. Most millionaires say their spouse was a huge reason for their financial success. Communicate with them each month about how to set next month's budget.

15. Review your Social Security statement. Check your work history for accuracy, making sure to compare to tax returns or pay stub/advice. Review the calculation of your benefit at ages 62, 65, and 70, in today's dollars and in future dollars (adjusted for inflation). The future dollar calculator on ssa.gov is excellent. Learn how ssa.gov calculates your benefit, which uses your highest thirty-five years of earnings (indexed/adjusted for inflation). Of all the earnings you have made over the years, how much do you still have in your net worth statement?

16. <u>Compare your spending to the "average" American.</u> The idea is to live frugally. It's a balance—live for today but don't sacrifice tomorrow in the process. Compare your spending, both in absolute dollars and on a percentage basis to see how you compare to the "average" American. For example, the average American household spends almost $832 per month on food (groceries, eating out, etc.), or 10% of their income. How do you compare? Is this an opportunity for you to become more frugal?

    You'll need to be thrifty enough to save and invest 20% of your salary for retirement. Plus, the more you lower your expenses, the smaller nest egg you'll need in retirement. It's the classic win-win scenario. Don't be too stingy though—you need balance, which includes experiencing life today, as well as saving for tomorrow. Invest in experiences— save up and spend a little on a family vacation (e.g., visit a national park). Enjoy each season of your life (your kids are only young once). But don't let lifestyle creep rob you of a "great big beautiful tomorrow" (Brian Preston).

17. <u>Work hard.</u> I believe God designed us to work hard, to have a purpose, to enjoy the satisfaction of a job well done, to relish the fruits of our labor. Being lazy is not a recipe for success. The job market rewards hard work, integrity, humility, emotional intelligence, and a positive attitude.

18. <u>Keep learning.</u> Just because you may have finished high school or college doesn't mean you should stop learning. Read personal finance books (e.g., *The Millionaire Next Door*), watch personal finance channels on YouTube (e.g., *The Money Guy Show*), and read financial blogs (e.g., *Mr. Money Mustache*). This education will help you level up your personal finance knowledge. Personal finance success is 80% behavior and 20% knowledge. Don't skip leg day.

19. Choose your occupation wisely. Read the book *StrengthsFinder 2.0* by Gallup and Tom Rath. This book is interactive and will identify what occupations you are likely a good fit for. Around 75% of folks dislike their job. Don't just complain about it, do something about it! Find out what you're good at—your strengths, your passion. Maybe you're already living as frugally as you can. You can only reduce your expenses so far; maybe you need a higher paying job, one better suited to your strengths and abilities.

20. Make sure you get the right insurance. If you're married and have kids, you need to get some **term life insurance**, preferably when you're younger (and healthier), when it's less expensive. Make sure you have health insurance. Consider **disability insurance**. 58% of Americans will be disabled at some point in their working life. Consider an **umbrella policy**. Once you've accumulated some **assets**, you're vulnerable to litigation—basic car and homeowners' insurance don't provide much coverage in the event you get sued.

Finally, don't compare your personal finance journey to the proverbial Joneses' (living it up on their European vacation as seen on Instagram). Comparison is the thief of joy. While personal finance is a competition, you're not competing against your neighbor, you're competing against yourself!

HOMEWORK

Because personal finance is, well, personal, this book is interactive. It only helps if you apply the principles to your personal finance journey.

1) Complete the 14-question questionnaire at the beginning of the chapter. How'd you do?

2) Calculate your net worth (example in Figure 1) and compare it to *The Millionaire Next Door* formula (#8 above). You'll want to track your net worth at least once a year, maybe on January 1, to monitor your progress over time.

3) Review your Social Security earnings statement at ssa. gov. What are your total lifetime earnings? How does this compare to your current net worth?

4) Review Jimmy's 20 Wealth-Building Rules to Live By. Which ones do you agree with? Which ones do you disagree with? Why?

ASSETS	
house	$400,000
2014 toyota corolla	$6,000
2016 toyota camry	$8,000
furniture, appliances, etc.	$2,000
jewelry, coins, etc.	$2,000
checking	$1,000
car sinking fund	$1,000
savings	$1,000
high yield savings	$25,000
401k	$11,000
401K	$210,000
vacation sinking fund	$1,000
roth IRA	$165,000
brokerage - bridge	$500
brokerage - emerg. Fund	$1,600
health savings account	$-
total assets	$835,100
LIABILITIES	
1st mortgage house, 2.95%	$256,000
credit card	$3,000
medical bills	$1,200
	$-
bank of dad	$9,500
	$-
total liabilities	$269,700
NET WORTH	**$565,400**

Figure 1: Example Net Worth

Chapter 2

BUDGETING: FREEDOM OR STRAITJACKET?

"If your outgo exceeds your income, then your upkeep will be your downfall" —Bill Earle

I watched many an episode of *Dora the Explorer* when my son was much younger, frequently hearing "I'm the Map!" chanted repeatedly by Dora's helpful sidekick. The last refrain is much louder and with an added emphasis that, frankly, seems entirely unnecessary . . .

A **budget**, however, is a necessary tool—a road map to financial freedom. A budget isn't a restrictive straitjacket that keeps you from having any fun. It's actually a tool that helps direct your life energy to those priorities that help you along your personal financial journey. Rather than finishing each month and wondering where it all went, I want you to set a budget before the month starts to direct your army of dollar bills on where they should go. Send each one on a mission.

To be technical, setting a budget is a three-step process.

1) Set up a tool to track your expenses, preferably using some automation, like the EveryDollar app that I've been using for years. Use my example in Figure 2 to get you going. Start with your big, **fixed**

commitments: tithe (in my case), rent/mortgage, car payment, student loan payments, etc.

Next, list normal recurring life **expenses**: gasoline, electricity, natural gas, cell phone, water, internet, healthcare, groceries, and eating out. Finally, set up a few categories for discretionary items: clothing, personal care (e.g., haircuts), entertainment, and the ever popular miscellaneous. Track your expenses for at least three months before you make any changes.

2) Set some short- and medium-term goals. Chapters 3 and 4 discuss goals/references to help you set a preliminary budget for how much you should spend on your budget line items. Merely tracking your expenses isn't really telling your dollar bills where to go. It's just investigating a little to see where they went. Use your three months of history as a guide for how much to budget in each category.

Use the Bureau of Labor Statistics (BLS) Consumer Expenditure Survey Table (see Figure 4 in chapter 4) to locate your income range. Look to see how much your peers spend on these same categories. For example, maybe your peer group spends $625 each month on food, or about 10% of their disposable income/total expenses. That's a starting point for a preliminary goal—don't spend more than your peers in this category. Of course you *can* spend more in this category, but then you'll have to spend less somewhere else (i.e., whack-a-mole) to bring you back to your disposable income (i.e., take-home-pay). Continue to monitor your spending (from #1 above) after you set your initial budget, to ensure you don't overspend in a category.

3) Set your "real" budget. This involves spending less than you make, creating **margin** (income less expenses) in your budget to allow you to save and invest for the future. Set your finances on a path toward financial freedom. Maybe you can only save and invest 5% initially,

but keep adjusting your budget to create a more sustainable path to your **financial independence**.

You might want to make changes to accelerate your path. For example, you can:

- Sell your house so you can purchase one you can more easily afford (see chapter 5).

- Replace your car with a more economical choice (see chapter 6).

- Review your **credit card** and student loan payments, maybe they're crowding out other categories (see chapter 13).

- Seek a better-paying job if you have cut your expenses as far as you can (see chapter 8).

Make sure you communicate with your spouse each month to set the budget for the next month (before the month starts!). This will take time, but having a meeting each month will set you up for success. If you're single, find a close friend you trust to be your accountability partner. I don't want you to set out on this journey alone.

A budget is your ticket to living life on your terms, not someone else's. If we're not in control of our money, then our money is in control of us. Budgeting is balancing freedom and responsibility. *You can't have freedom without responsibility*. Setting up your budget to encourage **saving** and **investing** is the goal, but not the only goal. A budget should balance living your best life today while also saving for tomorrow.

I'm competitive by nature and saving can be something of an obsession, if you let it. Be **frugal**, but don't be **cheap**. **Frugal** is being efficient and spending wisely. Spending wisely on things and experiences you value (that bring you joy). Being **cheap** is being miserly

THE MIDDLE-CLASS MILLIONAIRE

toward others. Don't be a cheapskate—especially in how you treat others. For example, tipping. Leave a tip commensurate with the service you received. If someone is very attentive in their service, tip 20% or more.

Don't confuse **needs** and **wants**. Don't let your desire for the good life outstrip your means. You can't spend whatever you want whenever you want. You'll need to be responsible and spend less than you make. If you carry a credit card balance from month to month, you're not spending less than you make.

"People who win in life have to work hard and be intentional. You have to tell your money what you want it to do." —Rachel Cruze.

Common budgeting pitfalls

- <u>Giving up too easily.</u> It will take time to get used to the budgeting routine. It only works if you are intentional and stick with it. Don't worry if you go over budget in a few categories, or overall (for the first couple months). This is part of the learning and adjusting process. You can do it! (Rob Schneider). Plan for there to be significant changes in the first few months, especially in miscellaneous and unexpected expenses.

  The best way to deal with unexpected or lumpy expenses is via **sinking funds**. You can have individual sinking funds (e.g., a vacation, clothing, house repair) or one big sinking fund. See Figure 2 for an example budget, which includes a $100 budget for clothing each month. If you don't spend the monthly allotment on clothing, move the leftover money into a savings account (a sinking fund), for a later month when you need it. Clothing expenses

20

tend to be lumpy, especially if you have kids. They are usually heavy for a month or two coinciding with back-to-school season.

Another approach is to use a **zero-based budget** (each month has its own unique budget, not a carryover from the previous month). Using this approach requires that you anticipate the ups and downs of these lumpy expenses. With time and experience, you'll get better at setting up your budget each month. Unexpected expenses will occur, which is a good reason to have an **emergency fund**.

- Spending too much. If you spend too much during an early month, analyze which category caused you to go over. You might have a spending problem that you can address to get back to living on less than you make (see chapter 4 for some tips on lowering your expenses), or you might have an income problem (see chapter 8 on career tips).

- You and your spouse are wired differently. It's common for one spouse to naturally be a saver and the other a spender. Good communication is the key to avoid money being a source of stress in your marriage. I'll go from preachin' to meddlin' (as my father says) and suggest you have joint checking. You're on the same team. Your monthly budget should cover all the income and expenses from your household. There's no his and her money anymore. There's no I in team. You can have a certain amount of "fun" money for each spouse, but you'll need to include this in your monthly budget.

HOMEWORK

1) Schedule a meeting (each month) with your spouse or accountability partner and review budget template in figure 2. Make sure to meet before the month starts.

2) If you haven't done so, set up an app (e.g., EveryDollar) and link it to your checking account so you can start tracking your actual expenses for the next three months.

3) If you already have a good, working budget, compare your spending to the BLS percentage next to each category and see if there are any areas for improvement. We'll take a deeper dive into the **BLS Consumer Expenditure Survey Table** in chapter 4.

4) Once a year, look back on your income and spending and do a simplified income statement (Figure 3) to see where your paycheck goes.

Please note Figure 2 starts with take-home pay (disposable income). Automating your saving/investing is the best way to ensure you set aside enough for **retirement**/financial freedom. My recommendation is to strive for a 20% saving/investing rate (including any company contributions). Set up your saving and investing to automatically come out of your paycheck each month. We'll discuss saving and investing more in chapter 10.

DEC-24	MONTH				VARI-ANCE, GOOD/ (BAD)	
Income	budget	actual	%	BLS %		
Spouse A	$3,000	$3,025			$25	
Spouse B	$2,000	$1,995			$(5)	
miscellaneous	$500	$495			$(5)	
Total Income	$5,500	$5,515			$15	
Expenses/Deductions						
Tithe/charity	$(550)	$(550)	0%	3%	$-	
Mortgage/rent	$(1,250)	$(1,250)	0%	29%	$-	BLS includes furniture and household services
car payment	$(400)	$(400)	0%	6%	$-	
Gasoline	$(250)	$(225)	0%	4%	$25	
car insurance	$(100)	$(100)	0%	2%	$-	
misc. transportation	$(50)	$(65)	0%	4%	$(15)	BLS includes repairs, maintenance, and public transportation
electricity	$(100)	$(100)	0%	2%	$-	
cell phone	$(150)	$(150)	0%	2%	$-	
Water	$(75)	$(85)	0%	1%	$(10)	
Internet/TV	$(90)	$(90)	0%	1%	$-	
nat gas	$(100)	$(100)	0%	1%	$-	
Groceries	$(500)	$(505)	0%	7%	$(5)	
Eat Out	$(300)	$(295)	0%	5%	$5	
savings	$(500)	$(500)	0%	9%	$-	
entertainment	$(200)	$(275)	0%	3%	$(75)	
healthcare	$(250)	$(245)	0%	7%	$5	
clothing	$(100)	$(95)	0%	2%	$5	
Life/Dis.Ins.	$(100)	$(100)	0%	1%	$-	
misc	$(400)	$(350)	0%	11%	$50	BLS includes personal pension
Total Expenses	$(5,465)	$(5,480)			$(15)	
checking balance 11/30/24		$3,000				
checking balance 12/31/24		$3,035				

Figure 2: Example Budget

GROSS PAY 2024		
Spouse 1	$75,000	
Spouse 2	$24,000	
Miscellaneous	$1,000	
	$100,000	
Taxes	$(6,860)	7%
Healthcare premiums/HSA	$(5,000)	5%
401k employee contributions	$(10,000)	10%
Misc. pre-tax	$(500)	1%
Take home pay	$77,640	78%
Food	$(9,600)	10%
Housing	$(25,000)	25%
Church/charity	$(6,600)	7%
Telecom/cable/entertainment	$(3,480)	3%
Transportation/gasoline	$(9,600)	10%
Medical/insurance	$(4,200)	4%
Misc.	$(6,000)	6%
Emergency fund	$(10,000)	10%
Roth IRA	$(3,160)	3%
check figure, should be zero	$-	100%
Retirement contributions (employer/employee)		$(23,160)
Retirement contribution %		23%

Figure 3: Simplified Income Statement

Chapter 3

WHAT ARE YOUR GOALS?
THINK BIG!

Your financial dream—this is the fun part. Go ahead and dream, but make sure you *dream BIG!* Let your imagination go. What do you want your financial future to look like? Does it involve debt? Harassing calls from collectors? **Living paycheck to paycheck**? (That's not a dream, that's a nightmare!)

To have the motivation to achieve your dream, you need to establish why you have the specific dream you have; otherwise, you might give up when times get tough, and they will get tough.

"You hungry for failure? Maybe a side of unemployment? 'Cause that's what's for lunch," Wolf inquires rhetorically in the movie *Hoodwinked.*

Setting goals is an important step on your **financial independence** journey. Setting goals is part of the planning process. It sets your priorities.

Try not to think about your **expenses** in terms of money, but rather in terms of time. Think about how much you make per hour and how much of your time is devoted to repaying debt. Time is finite (at least in this lifetime); you only have 24 hours in a day. You're not spending your money, you're spending your life energy. Consider the **opportunity cost**. Are you delaying your financial independence by borrowing from your future? How much of your **retirement** are you spending now? Consider that $500 per month car payment you'll be handing over for the next five years; that could've become $1,000,000 in your **retirement account** if you had invested that same $500 per month instead of purchasing that SUV that caught your eye.

For many, paying off debt is their number 1 financial priority. I certainly agree with that priority, but I would ask a basic question—WHY? I would say because most people want **financial stability** and the ability to build wealth. The best way to have financial stability and to build **wealth** is to be debt-free!

Maybe you want to be debt-free in order to save up for that dream home. Maybe you want to help others during your retirement. Maybe you want the peace of mind that comes from being debt-free, true financial peace. Imagine what that might be like—no debt payments to anyone! Give that a minute to soak in. Paint the picture; burn that image into your frontal cortex.

Regardless of your specific dream, being debt-free is a tailwind at your back because your ultimate goal will be that much easier to achieve without the burden and stress of debt.

I believe the first step in any successful financial process should be to establish an **emergency fund** of at least $1,000. This is a critical first step because an unexpected expense could derail that wonderful dream. The dream is not to have a home with a leaking roof and no money to repair it. I want it to be more than a dream though (dreams only come true in the movies); I want it to be a goal—a goal with steps, milestones, and, most importantly, a plan! (a.k.a. a **budget**).

Let's set some S.M.A.R.T. goals (to get out of debt) that are:

Specific
Measurable
Achievable
Relevant
Time-Bound

I want you to start with the end-goal in mind and work backward (I know that sounds crazy but stick with me). Conventional wisdom says you need to accumulate 25 times your annual retirement expenses to achieve financial independence, which is defined as the freedom to stop working if you so choose. For starters, you could use 70% of your pre-retirement salary as an estimate of your retirement income need.

Let's stick with that 25 times goal (at least for now) and then decide when you want to achieve your personal financial independence day. Let's start with twenty years as an example. My estimate of my annual retirement expenses is $80,000. Twenty-five times $80,000 is $2 million. This strategy assumes you could then stop working and withdraw 4% of the $2 million to "produce" a salary of $80,000 going forward (the so called **4% safe withdrawal rate**).

So if you want to accumulate $2 million in twenty years, how much do you need to save to get there? Let's assume that you earn an annual **rate-of-return** of 10%. Let's also assume you have already saved $250,000. If you save $12,000 per year, or $1,000 per month (about $33 per day), then you will have more than $2.4 million in twenty years! (That's the power of **compounding**). I hope you get the point of working backward to see how much you should be saving per month—or even per day; $33 per day sounds a lot more reasonable than trying to find an extra $12,000 per year.

If you need some help getting to your monthly savings goal, start by examining the big three expenses in your budget: housing, transportation, and food. I realize most of you have other expenses, but these three are usually between 60% and 70% of your expenses and are probably the most likely to be impacted by your personal choices.

You might also consider a side gig/hustle. I know it's not exciting, but you could deliver pizzas on weekends to earn some extra money. Getting ahead isn't easy, but as Dave Ramsey says, "If you will live like no one else now, later, you can live and give like no one else!"

Maybe we should stop using the word retire, or at least redefine it. Retirement shouldn't be defined by your age. If you work hard, you could be financially independent in twenty years and choose to keep working. That's freedom. Keep working at a job you love because you *want to*, not because you *have to*!

But let's say you made a few mistakes while playing the game of life and now you have accumulated some debts (e.g., student loans, car payments). What do you do now? You get mad and pay off those debts as fast as you can. Don't spend your life constantly paying off past debts. Pay off the smallest debt, then move on to the next one, and so on. I know it's not easy—getting ahead never is—but it will be worth it!

What motivates you?

I can't answer that question for you, but I can answer it for me. My 18-year-old son has autism. To provide for his medical and educational needs, I had to, and still continue to have to, get my finances right. I have a biblical responsibility to care for my son, and I'm sure I don't always get it right, but being a good parent is something that drives me to do my best each day.

For me, personal finance is . . . well . . . *personal*.

HOMEWORK

1) Write down your one, five, ten, and twenty-year goals using S.M.A.R.T. parameters. Make sure you write them down because

strategy without action is delusion. Post your goals somewhere visible to you each day; otherwise you'll get distracted and easily forget. Regularly discuss your goals with your spouse or accountability partner. They will likely change over time, so periodically revisit them. Don't forget to measure your progress!

I'll share a couple of my five-year goals: be totally debt-free by age 56. Quit my corporate gig and replace it with a part-time passion project (probably becoming a personal finance coach).

2) Work backward. What actions do you need to take each month to achieve your goals?

Don't try to do all this homework in one sitting. Start small and list some achievable one-year goals. They shouldn't all be financial, but most goals have financial consequences. I strongly encourage you to make improving your health and exercising a goal. Maybe you want better relationships with your immediate family. Maybe you need to prioritize your mental well-being. I humbly suggest you join a local church community—you need to be part of a caring community.

And don't set goals that are too aggressive. I want you to enjoy each season of your life, even if that means setting simple goals to help "bedazzle" your current lifestyle. Maybe you're living on a college student budget in your thirties to achieve your financial goals. Maybe you're paying off some **credit card debt**. Don't let that prevent you from saving up and taking a staycation with your family. Spend money on experiences in your home state.

Be sure to celebrate goal milestone achievements. Invite friends and family to join you on your financial freedom journey. You're not alone.

Chapter 4

HOW MUCH SHOULD
YOU PAY FOR THAT?

When building a **budget** or comparing your budget to what you *should* spend on certain categories, it's helpful to have some reference points. You're not competing against your neighbors in the game of personal finance; however, it might be helpful to look at a classmate's paper and see how they spend their hard-earned money.

The Bureau of Labor Statistics (BLS) spends your tax dollars on some pretty interesting reports. Some of these reports show how the "average" American spends their money.

Let's start with the **BLS Consumer Expenditure report**. See Figure 4 for the 2023 summary report (released in Q4 2024). You can also visit the BLS website for more details (e.g., average cell phone bill, average restaurant spend, etc.). Go to bls.gov / cex, select CE data, then Tables, then scroll down to find the specific income before taxes data you're looking for. (I prefer the Excel version, but there is also a PDF version).

Note the summary table below, figure 4, is categorized by household income ranges and major expenditure categories. Each category includes the total dollars spent annually, as well as the percentage each category represents, as a percentage of their total **expenses**. For example, the $150,000–$199,000 income group spent an average of $15,264 ($1,272 monthly) on food in 2023, or 13% of their total expenses.

The major expenditure categories are:

- Food
- Housing
- Apparel and Services
- Transportation
- Healthcare
- Entertainment
- Miscellaneous
- Cash contributions
- Personal Insurance

Table 1203. Income before taxes: Annual expenditure means, shares, Consumer Expenditure Surveys, 2023 only select columns shown					
Item		**$50,000 to $69,999**	**$70,000 to $99,999**	**$100,000 to $149,999**	**$150,000 to $199,999**	**$200,000 and more**
Food						
	Mean	8,413	9,705	11,960	15,264	18,525
	Share	14.1%	13.5%	13.2%	13.0%	10.6%
Alcoholic beverages						
	Mean	384	512	838	1269	1567
	Share	0.6%	0.7%	0.9%	1.1%	0.9%
Housing						
	Mean	21,164	24,424	28,405	34,505	51,055
	Share	35.6%	34.0%	31.3%	29.3%	29.2%
Apparel and services						
	Mean	1,339	2,111	2,467	3,014	4,671
	Share	2.3%	2.9%	2.7%	2.6%	2.7%
Transportation						
	Mean	10,437	12,634	16,653	21,137	28,308
	Share	17.6%	17.6%	18.4%	17.9%	16.2%
Healthcare						
	Mean	5,479	6,028	7,251	8,061	10,711
	Share	9.2%	8.4%	8.0%	6.8%	6.1%
Entertainment						
	Mean	2,309	3,167	3,998	5,879	9,526
	Share	3.9%	4.4%	4.4%	5.0%	5.4%
Personal care products and services						
	Mean	737	1020	1143	1409	1905
	Share	1.2%	1.4%	1.3%	1.2%	1.1%
Reading						
	Mean	98	94	157	173	242
	Share	0.2%	0.1%	0.2%	0.1%	0.1%
Education						
	Mean	813	1,106	1,253	2,109	6,804
	Share	1.4%	1.5%	1.4%	1.8%	3.9%
Tobacco products and smoking supplies						
	Mean	456	432	375	324	221
	Share	0.8%	0.6%	0.4%	0.3%	0.1%
Miscellaneous						
	Mean	1,400	1,079	1,307	1,758	2,375
	Share	2.4%	1.5%	1.4%	1.5%	1.4%
Cash contributions						
	Mean	1,905	1,942	2,398	c/	6,461
	Share	3.2%	2.7%	2.6%	c/	3.7%
Personal insurance and pensions						
	Mean	4,527	7,644	12,472	18,754	32,623
	Share	7.6%	10.6%	13.8%	15.9%	18.6%

c Data are suppressed due to the Relative Standard Error (RSE) being equal to or greater than 25 percent.

Source: Consumer Expenditure Surveys, U.S. Bureau of Labor Statistics, September, 2024

Figure 4: BLS Summary by Category

This report is a great way to see how much others spend on certain expenses. It's a good starting point if you've never established a **budget**. I especially like the **Age of Reference Person by Income Before Taxes** table because you can narrow your comparison to others in your same age category, which makes the comparison more relevant. A millennial's expenses will be quite different from that of a baby boomer who recently retired. Pick your respective age category and find out what your cohorts spend on life's normal, everyday expenses.

A word of caution: The BLS survey is what the "average" person spends. This proverbial "average" person isn't meant to be held up as some kind of ideal. Quite the contrary, this "average" person is really the C student in school. It's a useful reference to see how a C student did on the test, but I wouldn't celebrate too much if you're level with, or slightly better than, a C student (Don't celebrate mediocrity!). Conversely, don't console yourself if you're only *slightly worse* than this proverbial C student.

I'm in the 45-54 category so I'll use that as my reference point (see Figure 5). Choose *your respective age cohort* and consider why are you doing better or *worse* than "average." If you are below average, then you should absolutely sit around the kitchen table and ponder, "How can I improve?" Enough small talk, let's get to the numbers!

TABLE 3234, CONSUMER EXPENDITURE SURVEYS			
2022-2023			
Age 45-54, greater than $100,000 column			
Food (includes alcohol)		$1,482	
	groceries		$761
	restaurants (includes alcohol)		$722
Housing		3,143	
	mortgage (incl. prop taxes and ins)		$1,322
	utilities		$540
	household operations		$210
	household furnishings		$383
	housekeeping supplies		$102
	other lodging		$586
Transportation		$1,847	
	car payment (including financing)		$830
	gasoline		$382
	insurance		$224
	repairs/maintenance		$142
	other		$268
Healthcare		$725	
Entertainment		$568	
	pets		$128
	TV/streaming		$122
	admissions, concerts, movies, etc.		$186
	other		$131
Life insurance/disability/ social security tax		$1,887	
Miscellaneous		$1,047	
cash contributions		$349	
total monthly expenses		$11,048	

Figure 5: BLS Summary by Age of Reference Person Per Month Spend

Food. We spent $1,555 *per month* on food in 2023. That's higher than the reference of $1,482, which is the food/groceries number from the BLS report. Our food and groceries expense is modified to include personal care items (e.g., shaving cream), and household goods (e.g., laundry detergent). We buy most of our groceries at Walmart, including things like shampoo and laundry detergent; we don't account for these items separately. The BLS categorizes these last items as miscellaneous (personal care), and housing (laundry detergent). I believe it's pretty easy to diagnose my problem here—it's going out to eat! I know I should bring my lunch to work most days and should avoid restaurants, *especially desserts* . . .

Housing. This includes anything and everything associated with the house, including: mortgage payment(s), property taxes, property insurance, utilities, household items, repairs, maintenance, furniture, appliances, etc. (you get the idea). Let's break this down into a couple of components:

- Our monthly mortgage payment in 2023 was $1,420, which includes property taxes and insurance. I believe the comparable BLS number is $1,886 (including $564 in principal payments – a footnote in BLS table), but that might be a touch high due to their inclusion of household maintenance, which my mortgage payment doesn't include. I estimate my repairs/maintenance/renovation at 1% annually. When I include an additional 1% in my monthly figure, then I'm pretty close to the BLS number of $1,886.

- Our monthly utilities were $402. The BLS comparable number is $540.

Transportation. Let's try rapid fire. Our car payment is $0 per month (woo-hoo!). BLS shows a car payment of $830 (whoa Nellie!). We spent $304 per month on gasoline (BLS average is $382). Maybe my best category . . .

I spent a little more on **healthcare** and quite a bit more on charity than the BLS. But I spent about the same on TV. I think you get the idea. Plug in your numbers and see if you're doing better or worse than the BLS averages.

I know this exercise seems detailed (a.k.a. boring!), but sometimes personal finance involves a little number crunching and critical thinking about how you can spend less.

If you have never followed a budget before, this is a great opportunity to get started. Today! Don't wait! This BLS template is not perfect, but I do think it's a good place to begin.

The BLS table is incredibly long and contains a ridiculous amount of data, but it's a really helpful resource because it makes it easier to compare your household spending to households of similar income, and how they prioritize their spending.

Again, I am not saying these reference points are the "correct" level of spending. In many cases, I would argue their priorities are a little wonky; nonetheless, it should help you in analyzing your own finances. While you'll likely rate better than average in some areas, you'll probably fall below in others, which is an opportunity to improve and set new goals. I know I am motivated to reduce the amount I spend on food.

Ways to Reduce Your Monthly Expenses

Now that you've learned how your neighbors prioritize their spending, let's pivot and think about ways to reduce *your* monthly expenses. Creating **margin** in your budget is one of the most effective ways to be able to save and invest for the future. One way to create additional margin is by reducing your recurring expenses.

Below are my Top 5 Ideas (plus 5 more bonus ideas) to help you reduce your monthly recurring expenses.

All these ideas might not apply to your situation, but I tried to choose expenses that you most likely have on a monthly/recurring basis; these are also areas that I have personally saved money (except for Stitch Fix and ShoeDazzle—I know, I know . . . that's just crazy talk!).

1. Food – Eat out less, bring your lunch to work, and shop smarter for groceries—try Aldi, Lidl, or Walmart.

2. Heating and cooling – Use programmable thermostats, fans, and a little extra caulk and insulation. (See later in this chapter for specific ideas.)

3. TV bill – Go with Netflix and free over-the-air broadcasts.

4. Insurance – Swap that expensive whole life policy with a less expensive term life policy.

5. Vacation – Research less expensive places to stay (Mickey gets paid too much anyhow.)

5 more bonus ideas

1. Drop that gym membership. – (You hardly ever use it); ride your bike, work out at home.

2. Reduce the monthly security bill. – There are less expensive options compared to those big security companies.

3. Get your java fix at home. – Stop buying that latte from Starbucks! Make your coffee at home.

4. Skip Stitch Fix and ShoeDazzle.

5. Unsubscribe from Spotify Premium or Apple Music. – Listen to the radio or get the ad-supported version of Spotify (free!).

I'd like to elaborate on how I trimmed my monthly heating and cooling expenses without sacrificing comfort. I really do enjoy AC , especially during the dog days of summer, which are pretty oppressive in North Carolina.

Here, in the southern piedmont of NC, we spent $2,731 on heating and cooling in 2023, or about $228 per month (2,426 square feet, built in 1996, electric for AC, natural gas for heat). I get a monthly report from Duke Energy that shows how my electric usage compares to the mythological "efficient" home. I'm so competitive that I have to be better than this "efficient" home. (Channel your inner LL Cool J.)

I work for a utility company, so this is an area I'm passionate about (if you couldn't already tell). Here are some of the things I have done—mostly as suggestions from one of our internal HVAC-licensed energy auditors:

- I made an attic tent out of plywood and silver insulation to cover the pull-down stairs opening leading to the attic of our two-story house. Pull-down stairs are rarely insulated and are one of the biggest areas of lost energy in a typical home.

- I caulked around all my windows to prevent the air from sneaking in or out. This was not done during construction, which may be the case for you too.

- I put silver insulation backing on the door to the eaves, similar to the attic tent.

- I added outlet gaskets to insulate all my outside facing walls. They are inexpensive, only about $0.25 each. Outlets are rarely insulated.

- I installed programmable thermostats. Buy them and use them! If you are going to be gone for eight hours or more (e.g., while at work), raise the temp (in the summer) at least five degrees (I don't recommend more than ten); lower in the winter. We set it at 77 during the day (when we are away) and 72 at night. We program differently for Monday through Friday than Saturday and Sunday since we are home more on the weekends.

- Install ceiling fans in areas where you spend most of your time. For us, this is the bonus room. Fans don't help heat or cool, but they do make us feel warmer in the winter and cooler in the summer (counterclockwise in summer, clockwise in winter).

We spent about $200–$300 on these projects, with the ceiling fan being the most expensive—note, we already had the programmable thermostats. These are all DIY projects, so we didn't hire any of these projects out.

HOMEWORK

1. Compare your spending, by income category, to the BLS Consumer Expenditure Survey (published annually each September at bls.gov). Are there categories you could improve in? These are opportunities.

2. List your opportunities and then make a plan to make it happen. If you don't track your expenses, then your homework assignment is to start today (yes, I said today!). Try an automated service like the EveryDollar app.

Chapter 5

HOUSING OPTIONS

Half your income for rent? *The New York Times* reports that 44 million American households rent their home. Of those renting, almost half (22 million) are considered "burdened" because their rent is over 30% of their pre-tax income. One in four (10 million) are paying over 50% of their pre-tax income on rent—"severely burdened." Craziness I say! According to Zillow, 21% is the historical "norm."

Housing affordability is at the lowest level in history (2024). This is due in part to high prices—the home market is undersupplied and labor and materials are higher due to inflation and increasing regulations—and high interest rates on mortgages. High interest rates also affect renters because developers have to pay higher interest costs, which are passed along to renters.

Per *The Wall Street Journal*, average rent is over $2,000 per month, while the average mortgage is over $3,000 per month. Before the FED started raising interest rates, a person with a monthly housing **budget** of $2,000 could have purchased a home valued at over $400,000. Now, that same buyer would need to find a home valued at $295,000 or less in order to maintain their $2,000 monthly budget. In 1980, the average home cost $64,000, while the average household income was $21,020. So the average home was three times the average annual income. In 2023, the average home was $431,000 while the average household income was $74,580. The average home nowadays is close to six times the average annual income. Craziness I say!

Year	Average Household Income	Average Home Cost	Housing Cost Relative to Income
1980	$21,020	$64,000	3.0
2023	$74,580	$431,000	5.8

Figure 6: Housing Affordability

I want to give you some tools and ideas to help evaluate if you should rent or buy, and how much of your income you should allocate to your monthly housing expense. If you don't have a plan, you could find yourself stuck in a vicious cycle—not **saving** enough for a down payment to purchase a home and, therefore, forced to keep paying ever-increasing rental payments. This could lead to **living paycheck to paycheck, credit card debt**, etc.

In most major markets, buying a home is a better long-term solution (versus renting), but only if you're ready. Let's ask some questions first . . .

Are you ready to buy a home?

Do you plan to stay in your home less than five years? This might be a difficult question, but you will need to give it your best guess. If you said yes, you should probably rent; the transaction costs of buying and selling a home are too high if you move frequently.

How much time and money are you willing to spend on repairs and maintenance? This is especially important if you are interested in purchasing a single-family home rather than a condo or townhouse. Moneyzine recommends estimating 1% of the purchase price for annual repairs and maintenance on your new home. The problem with home repairs and maintenance is that they are lumpy—they don't occur on a regular basis. For example, it's difficult to know when major appliances (furnace, air conditioner) will fail, or when the roof might spring a leak. These **expenses** will surely occur. It's wise to set aside money monthly into a housing fund that can be used to pay for these irregular but inevitable **expenses**.

You might ask yourself how handy you are, and if you have time to do repairs and maintenance. If you don't want that inconvenience, then maybe you should opt for a townhouse or condo, whereby the homeowners association is usually responsible for exterior maintenance. Just remember, you're paying for this convenience, usually via high monthly Homeowners' Association (HOA) dues.

<u>What is the comparison in rent versus a mortgage in your part of the country?</u> Do some research. Look at comparable homes in your area—both for sale and for rent. Add up the monthly expenses for interest, property taxes, and insurance. This is the rental portion of a monthly mortgage payment. Ignore the principal portion of your payment (for this exercise); housing prices increase at basically the same rate as inflation (over long periods of time), so it's extremely likely that you will sell your house for more than you originally paid for it. Compare the rental portion of your monthly mortgage payment with a comparable house. Also factor in that your rent is likely to go up over time—probably in line with inflation; however, it has jumped 4%–5% in some areas. Just sayin'.

I will share my situation:

$614 monthly interest (goes down over time)

$377 monthly escrow (property taxes and insurance) (goes up over time)

$355 monthly repairs and maintenance (using the 1% factor) (goes up over time)

$1,346 total

When I looked up comparably sized houses for rent in my zip code, I found a range of homes listed for $2,000–$2,400 in monthly rent. Realize that the landlord is paying comparable expenses too: property taxes, insurance, principal, interest, repairs and maintenance—*as well as making a profit.* I'm saving about $700—$1,100 per month by owning rather than renting. It probably helps that I've lived in the same house for the past nineteen years.

In most markets, the rental portion of your mortgage will probably be less than a comparable house would rent for. However, you have to use this savings to "offset" the up-front mortgage costs: appraisal, loan origination, realtor fees, etc., which could easily be $3,000–$5,000. A portion of this savings will also be used for repairs and maintenance; use 1% of the purchase price as an annual estimate.

When you compare buying versus renting in your area, you might find you can rent a home for less **cash flow** each month versus buying. Some encourage you to then rent and invest the difference between renting and buying. In theory, this is a valid strategy. If you rent a single-family home for $2,000 versus a comparable $3,000 mortgage, then you would need to invest $1,000 each month (e.g., in an **S&P 500 index**). In actuality though, I think this strategy has some flaws. First, it would take tremendous discipline to invest $1,000 each month; but you could automate this via a bank draft. Second, that $2,000 rent is going to go up over time (when your lease renews each year), while the mortgage is fixed (principal and interest component). Plus, the principal payment portion of your mortgage is building equity (i.e., forced saving). Finally, a house will appreciate at the rate of inflation (normally). Personally,

I would be willing to pay a little more to purchase a home rather than rent because I believe in the long run, purchasing is a better avenue toward building **wealth**.

Renting vs. Buying Conclusion

Ultimately it's not overly important (financially) whether you rent or purchase your home. I do suggest you limit your housing expense to 25% (no more than 30%) of your pre-tax income. I believe limiting your housing expense to 25% gives you the best chance to succeed, by saving and **investing**. If your housing expense is 50%, you likely will find it very difficult to find room in your budget to save and invest.

I believe that purchasing is better than renting (financially at least) over the long run (most of the time anyhow). You can also make home improvements/decorating decisions without getting the approval of the landlord; plus, you might be able to deduct the interest and property taxes on your income tax return (if you itemize). The landlord is going to set the rent at a level to cover his costs as well as make some profit. If you would rather rely on the landlord for needed repairs and maintenance, then you are *going to ultimately pay for that—via rent*. This concept applies to pretty much any convenience in life.

Let's illustrate what 25% looks like with an example (see Figure 7), using a household income of $100,000:

Household income	$100,000
Divided by 12	$8,333
Times 25%	$2,083
House purchase price	$325,000
Less 20% down payment	$(65,000)
Financed portion	$260,000
30-year mortgage at 5%	
Principal & interest	$1,400
Homeowners' Insurance	$167
Property taxes	$167
Utilities	$300
Total housing expense	$2,034
Housing cost % of income	24%

Figure 7: 25% Housing Illustration

Maybe you think 25%–30% of your income for housing sounds great, but when you look at prices in your area, the math just doesn't work—everything is too expensive!

Here's some practical, but not necessarily easy or convenient, advice:

- Get a roommate to reduce your costs.

- Expand your geographic area. The most popular parts of town usually have exceptionally high prices for real estate.

- Consider a different occupation/career. Maybe your income is too low for you to afford a home no matter how **frugal** you are.

- Select a townhouse or condo, especially for your first home. A condo or townhouse is typically going to be more affordable than a single-family house. But watch out for high HOA fees.

- Start with a tiny home. I know this sounds a little extreme, but consider this a sacrifice to save up for a down payment on your dream home. Your first house doesn't have to be your "forever" house.

- Shop around, especially if you are renting. Don't just accept a price increase from the landlord; use the internet and look for a better price. It's cheaper (and more convenient) to at least attempt to negotiate with your current landlord; good tenants are hard to find. Leverage that fact into a better price.

- Go on social media and ask for suggestions. Maybe someone you know has a room for rent.

- Don't buy more house than you need. Although purchasing a home might be financially beneficial over time, it doesn't compare favorably to the returns you could get in a low-cost index fund (invested in the **stock market**). Buy as much house as you need and invest the rest!

15-year versus 30-year mortgage

If you decide you want to purchase a home, let's consider three options: cash, a 15-year mortgage, or a 30-year mortgage (see Figure 8).

	Home Price	6.80% Interest Cost	Total Purchase Price	Monthly Payment	Annual Income Needed For 25% Rule
Cash	430,000	N/A	430,000	N/A	N/A
15-year mortgage	430,000	257,067	687,067	3,817	183,216
30-year mortgage	430,000	579,180	1,009,180	2,803	134,544

Figure 8: 15-Year vs. 30-Year Mortgage

If you buy a home for $430,000 (average price in 2023), and you pay cash, your purchase price is $430,000 (thanks Captain Obvious). Let's assume you don't have enough cash to pay for it up-front and have to finance it. Banks offer two main options: a 15- or 30-year mortgage. We'll assume no down payment for simplicity and comparison purposes.

That same $430,000 house will cost you $687,067 as you make 180 monthly payments of $3,817. The $687,067 purchase price includes $257,067 in interest cost at a 6.8% interest rate. Maybe you say, I can't afford a monthly payment of $3,817 because our household income isn't $183,216. Let's review the 30-year mortgage option because it comes with a lower monthly payment.

That same $430,000 house will now cost $1,009,180 (oh my!) as you make 360 monthly payments of $2,803. The $1,009,180 purchase price includes $579,180 in interest cost at a 6.8% interest rate. $579,180 is more than the original purchase price! This analysis is why I think you should at least consider a 15-year mortgage.

One other trick you should consider. If you choose a 30-year mortgage and make one extra principal payment per year, it shortens your mortgage to a 25-year mortgage.

Final comments on purchasing

Your first home isn't likely going to be your forever home. I suggest you start with a condo or townhouse that you can afford. Remember, your housing expense should be 25% of your gross income. This allows you the **margin** in your budget to save and invest 20% toward **retirement**. I also suggest you use a **credit union** to finance your mortgage. Credit unions usually have lower interest rates than the big banks. Plus, they usually don't charge **private mortgage insurance (PMI)** (if your down payment is less than 20%).

Especially on your first home, it's OK to put down less than 20%, even as little as 3% or 5%. In chapter 13, I recommend a 15-year mortgage to reduce your overall interest expense and to pay off your debt sooner rather than later. However, it's more realistic to assume you'll get a 30-year mortgage on your first home. The goal is to create margin in your budget to save and invest for the future.

Should you spend your hard-earned money on home renovations?

What does the cost-benefit analysis look like? Our home is over twenty years old, and there are many areas that are starting to show some age. For example, our kitchen is pretty dated. Yes, we watch too much HGTV.

I realize that *Fixer Upper* is just a TV show (we love Chip and Joanna), but watching this got me to thinking about whether or not it's smart to spend hard-earned money on home improvements. Maybe you recently received a tax refund (national average is over $3,000) or a bonus and are wondering if you should invest some of that in your largest investment—your home?

Before you consider a renovation project, calculate your total housing expense as a percentage of your income. If it's greater than 30%, then you should consider downsizing to properly fit your budget (ideally 25% of your income or less).

Another important consideration when contemplating a home renovation is whether or not your current home meets your family's needs. Maybe your family is larger now. Moving to a different home might be more economical than a major renovation.

Let me start this analysis off by giving a nod to financial expert Dave Ramsey and encourage everyone to properly budget for any home improvements they want to tackle. I don't want that nice kitchen remodel to be financed via a home equity loan. Your renovation idea might be a great investment—more on that later in the chapter—but I want you to eventually be debt-free. Don't try to borrow your way to prosperity by "investing" in a $20,000 gourmet kitchen. Enough small talk, should I spend some of my hard-earned money on updating my twenty-something-year-old home (or not)?

It depends on three things:

1. <u>How long do you plan to stay in your home?</u> The answer to this question will probably determine how much you should spend and what priorities you should have. If you plan to stay put for a few years, then keep reading. If you plan to sell your home in the next couple of years, only do minimal updates at the advice of your realtor.

2. <u>Is this improvement going to make your life better?</u> Think of the improvement to your current situation as the dividend that this "investment" pays.

3. <u>Will this improvement increase the value of the home when you eventually sell it?</u> I encourage you to walk through your home and objectively evaluate which areas are significantly out-of-date, especially relative to houses in your neighborhood. I encourage you to observe your neighbors' homes. Have most updated their kitchens to granite or quartz countertops? If they have—and you still

have the original laminate from twenty or thirty years ago—then this might be a big negative to a would-be buyer. I suggest hiring a professional interior designer to evaluate your home, or have a realtor friend come by and give you some free advice on what potential buyers in your area expect, before you consider a major renovation project.

If your home is over twenty years old, it's probably also worth paying for another inspection to see if there are any significant repairs that will necessarily precede any nice-to-have improvement projects you're dreaming of.

Following are some suggested improvements at different price points from a *USA Today* article (NerdWallet). I think these ideas will potentially make your life better today, as well as attract a would-be buyer in the future. A few small renovations might turn your starter home into your forever home. Realize renovation costs will vary by location and preference. Use this list as the beginning of a brain-storming session to freshen up your current house.

$300–$500

Replace cabinet hardware. Changing knobs or handles is a pretty simple DIY project and gives your cabinets a fresh, updated look. Maybe you have some outdated brass hardware—consider something more modern to spruce up your kitchen. I allocated $500 for this update but you could do it less expensively (maybe as low as $200), but you could also spend more; choose wisely.

$700–$1,000

Add a tile backsplash. A backsplash is much less expensive than a full kitchen remodel but can significantly change the look and feel of your kitchen.

Refresh interior paint. New paint in some of the main rooms can really brighten up the whole house—and doing the work yourself can substantially reduce the cost of this project.

Insulate the attic. You can usually get a local insulation company to do a free evaluation of how much insulation you already have, and if you would benefit from additional insulation. You will enjoy lower utility bills, and would-be buyers love energy-efficient homes.

$1,500–$2,000

Tile a bathroom floor. You might still have the original laminate flooring that is showing its wear from heavy foot traffic. Opt for bright, easy-to-clean tile instead.

Get a new front door. A fiberglass door won't swell or contract like a wooden door. Consider painting it red for a fresh look as an upgrade to your curb appeal.

Replace inefficient appliances like an old water heater, refrigerator, or dishwasher. You will appreciate the newer, more efficient appliances, and would-be buyers will have one less thing to worry about when they move in.

$2,000–$3,000

Install new kitchen countertops. Almost all potential buyers want granite, quartz, or one of the solid surfaces. Plus, the kitchen is the most important room in evaluating a new home according to Zillow.

Replace the garage door. A new garage door recoups around 98% of its cost in improved home value. If you have the original white aluminum door, consider an upgrade to a carriage style with a stained wood look.

It will greatly increase the curb appeal and will most likely be more energy efficient as well.

Enhance your landscaping. Stone pavers, a fire pit, or exterior lighting could improve your curb appeal.

Most home improvements do not pay for themselves—via a higher sales price. However, they will likely impact if your home sells and *how quickly*. Some renovations manage to recover 80%–90% of their costs, while others barely cover half their cost (Bankrate.com). For this reason, I encourage you to pick projects that will enhance your current life—because you can't justify adding a fifth bedroom to your house merely as an "investment."

Don't upgrade beyond your neighborhood. Adding a pool might be unusual in your neighborhood and could be a detriment when trying to sell because you overimproved for your area. I recommend you invite a realtor to your home, one familiar with your area, to size it up and see if it has any significant flaws. These flaws are opportunities to improve the value of your home—both to you and to a potential future buyer.

If you decide to hire a contractor, shop around and ask friends for recommendations. Get references from the contractor and speak directly with them. I encourage you to get multiple quotes (three preferably) if you plan on spending more than $1,000.

Remember that most repairs and maintenance won't increase the resale value of your home. If you recently replaced a leaky roof or an old HVAC system don't expect to raise the selling price to cover those costs. It might actually hurt your resale price if you don't do these necessary repairs.

My advice is to focus on small projects that you can afford and that truly make your life better today. I recommend you focus on the kitchen, especially if it's out-of-date (like mine). Steer clear of big projects like an in-ground pool or a gourmet kitchen. These projects might involve debt and are probably poor investments.

HOMEWORK

1. Calculate your housing expense, mortgage/rent plus utilities, as a percentage of your income. Are you in the 25%–30% range?

2. Are there any changes you can/should make to reduce your housing expense?

3. Are there any opportunities to reduce your heating and cooling costs?

4. Are there any home improvements you should consider?

Chapter 6

CAR-BUYING STRATEGIES

C ars, cars, cars; I *really* like cars. And I'm not alone, most Americans do. According to the interwebs, we like them too much. The average car payment in 2023 was $726 (LendingTree) with an average loan of $40,184[1] over 68.3 months (that's over five-and-a-half years!). $533 is the average payment for used cars, financing $27,167 over 67.6 months.

Consider how much $726 invested over five-and-a-half years could be worth if you saved and invested that same amount of money and allowed it to grow from age 25 to 65 at a 10% **rate-of-return**. That same $726 monthly car payment would be worth $1.8 million at age 65. That new car didn't cost $40,184; it cost $1.8 million! This concept of the trade-off between alternative uses of $726 per month is called **opportunity cost**.

> Opportunity cost - the loss of potential gain from another possible choice. It is what you are giving up by spending money on one alternative versus another. If you spend $40,184 on a new car, you are forgoing the benefit of **investing**

---

[1] Lending Tree math doesn't appear to be the total payments: $726 monthly payment for 68.3 months is $49,585, which is greater than the $40,184 originally financed, due to interest.

that same \$40,184 in the **stock market**. That same \$40,184 could grow to \$1.8 million if allowed thirty-five years of **compounding** (10% interest). The opportunity cost is the thing you can no longer achieve because you chose to spend this money on something else. Always consider the alternatives you are giving up by committing to a purchase.

According to Statista, 38% of used cars are financed, and over 80% of new cars are financed. My philosophy is a little counter to conventional wisdom, but I hope you will indulge my strategy as you consider your options for your next vehicle.

Car payments are financial napalm to your **net worth** and your efforts to build **wealth** over time. Cars are a depreciating asset, meaning they lose value over time, and quite quickly at that. Per Edmunds, a new car loses 11% of its value the moment you drive it off the lot. They depreciate another 15%–25% each year after that. After five years, your new car is worth only 37% of the price you paid.

Jimmy's Top 5 Car-Buying Tips

1. Don't buy a new car. Unless your net worth is already in excess of \$1 million, I strongly advise you to buy a gently used car. This allows you to avoid the depreciation that occurs as soon as you drive it off the lot. This loss of value is quite excessive, especially the first couple of years of ownership.

2. Don't lease. Numerous studies, including Edmunds', have proven that this is the most expensive way to "finance" your transportation needs. There are a couple of exceptions (there usually are), but the average consumer shouldn't even consider a lease. It's simply too profitable for the dealerships/manufacturers. That's why they push leases so hard. Roughly 25% of consumers opt for a lease.

That's way too high! Be smarter about your next vehicle. It's also a convenient way for many to get a new car they really can't afford (by focusing only on the monthly payment). In short, don't sign a fleece—it's complicated, costs way too much, and greatly limits your options both during (e.g., mileage) and at the end of the lease (e.g., surrender value). Leases don't have to disclose the "real" interest rate, but it's estimated to be 14% (Dave Ramsey). Don't bet against the big car manufacturers—it's like betting against Vegas (the house almost always wins!). The big depreciation (loss in value) is "baked into" your lease payment.

3. Don't limit your focus to the monthly payment. Think about the life cycle cost—the total cost of ownership over the time that you own the vehicle. This includes: principal and interest payments, fuel, insurance, maintenance, depreciation, etc. Edmunds calls it "total cost to own." For starters, I recommend going to Edmunds.com and doing some research on any cars you are considering. Life cycle cost is the best way to measure the value. Remember, *price is what you pay, value is what you receive.*

4. Don't buy a vehicle you can't afford. Buy a car you can pay off in three years. 20/3/8—20% down, financed for no more than three years, payment no more than 8% of your salary. Another more aggressive guideline, per Moneyzine, is don't exceed 20% of your annual income on your next vehicle. For example, if your annual salary is $100,000, then you shouldn't spend more than $20,000 on your next vehicle. If your salary is $50,000, then aim for a $10,000 ride. This more aggressive approach might be unrealistic. I recommend following the 20/3/8 plan to

avoid spending too much on a depreciating asset—it's an expense not an investment! Over time, that new vehicle you bought will decrease your net worth. That's a deal you don't need!

5. <u>Do your research and buy a car that is reliable, safe, and relatively fuel efficient,</u> but make sure it suits your needs (e.g., don't buy a Suburban if you don't have any kids). I recommend starting with recommended vehicles from *Consumer Reports*. Research the make and model and choose vehicles with a record of being reliable and safe. *The Millionaire Next Door* says to avoid foreign luxury cars—instead opt for a domestic car that you can either pay cash for, or at least pay off in the next two-to-three years. Your vehicle isn't a piece of jewelry; it's a resource to safely get you from point A to point B.

5 more tips, because I'm that kinda guy:

1. <u>Buy your next vehicle from CarMax.</u> They aren't paying me for this endorsement—I'm just trying to save you from shady used car salespeople out there who don't have your best interest in mind. If not CarMax, then I recommend a certified used vehicle in order to ensure you aren't buying a repair nightmare. Don't buy somebody else's problem.

2. <u>Sell your current vehicle to CarMax.</u> They will buy your vehicle regardless of whether you purchase your next vehicle from them. This is cleaner and avoids any confusion that can occur when you trade in your vehicle. Do these two transactions separately and make a smart (non-emotional) decision both times. Do your research and determine the value of your existing vehicle. I

recommend checking out Edmunds (edmunds.com) or Kelley Blue Book (kbb.com) before you visit CarMax. And make sure to remove all your personal items and have the car professionally cleaned / detailed before you get their offer.

3. <u>Don't keep the vehicle too long and get some crazy high repair bills on an unreliable vehicle.</u> This could leave you in an unsafe situation (e.g., on the side of the road at night) and maybe result in missing work. Unreliable transportation is a ticket to losing your job and could turn out to be a financial disaster. Vehicles are designed to last ten years or about 200,000 miles. If you are careful and do the proper maintenance, you could possibly get fifteen years or 300,000 miles out of your vehicle. After that, however, you are borrowing trouble. Anticipate when this will occur and set aside money each month into a car fund so you can pay cash for your next purchase. It shouldn't be a surprise when your vehicle "expires." Adopt the Boy Scouts' motto—be prepared!

4. <u>Don't skip the required maintenance (including tires).</u> Read the manual and find out what the manufacturer recommends for maintenance. Follow the manufacturer's schedule, not the dealership's, who may recommend extra maintenance that only serves to add to their profits.

5. <u>If you realize you have a car that you can't afford, sell it!</u> Don't keep it. It will continue to depreciate. Sell it and buy a gently used car that you can afford. Remember the 20% annual salary target.

Final thoughts

Don't trade often. Keep your vehicle for at least five years, preferably six or seven. I personally would not spend more than the vehicle is worth on a repair. For example, if the Kelley Blue Book price for your vehicle is $1,000 and you encounter a $1,200 repair, scrap the car rather than invest more into a car than it's worth. Do the math—it might be better to sell the car as is.

If you have to finance your next vehicle, opt for a **credit union** loan (if you can); their rates and fees are usually much lower than the national banks. Try to pay off your car loan (insist on a simple interest loan) early (two-to-three years), and then start setting aside money each month for the next vehicle, so you can pay cash, in order to be debt-free!

HOMEWORK

1. Do you have a car payment? How does it compare to the 20/3/8 guideline above? If you are not following the 20/3/8 guideline, then maybe you need to sell that car and get a more affordable one.

2. When do you plan to buy your next car?

3. How do you plan to pay for the next car purchase?

4. What would you do if you had to buy your next car earlier than anticipated?

Chapter 7

LIFESTYLE CREEP

I t's one of the most common answers given by **millionaire**s as to how they achieved success—they avoided lifestyle creep. So what actually is lifestyle creep? According to Investopedia:

Lifestyle creep is when your standard of living rises alongside your discretionary income—and soon enough, former luxuries become new necessities. It happens little by little, without you really realizing it: it sneaks ("creeps") up on you.

I know I'm guilty—especially of going out to eat. When I was in college, Taco Bell was a staple: $0.29, $0.39, $0.49 tacos. I could eat lunch for under $2, and that usually involved four or five tacos. Dinner was frequently pizza. My two roommates and I would split a large pizza that only cost $5. Split three ways, that was a pretty good deal, even though the pizza wasn't really that good. More like marinara sauce on cardboard, but hey, I was on a college **budget** . . . Fast-forward to today. We spend over $700 per month going out to eat. I lost the college life-style and my budget conscious mindset—guess I thought I *deserved* to go out to nicer restaurants . . . (wrong!)

I've driven two Honda Civics (total of thirteen years combined) in the past, but today I drive a much nicer Chevy Impala. If I had chosen to continue living my **frugal** college lifestyle even after I started my career, I would have been able to save more and accelerate my **financial independence**. This is one of the secrets that millionaires have figured out. It takes a tremendous amount of self-control to delay gratification and keep driving that "old" car for a few more years. The benefits to your **saving**s are tremendous. Let's back up to when you first graduated from college.

Let's say your first job out of college paid a $50,000 salary and you learned to live on that. If you had banked your first raise and maintained your current standard of living, over time you would've saved a significant percentage of your salary.

So for those currently in this situation, this means holding onto your stuff longer: clothes, cars, smartphones, houses—you name it—hang onto it as long as you can and keep your **expenses** low. It's the secret sauce to getting ahead. It means you will want to research and buy quality items that will last. The cheapest clothes aren't necessarily the best value; in fact, they rarely are.

If you can invest 20% of your salary (without going into debt) and live on the rest, then you are fast on your way to financial success.

I want to add one more topic to this discussion—vacations. Just check Facebook and I'm sure you will see some amazing pictures of places your friends have gone recently. Don't compare your vacation to your social media feed. This unhealthy comparison is a competition you can't win. Don't compare your life to their social media avatar. What you may not realize is their **credit card** was maxed out for that two-week stay in Bermuda. Don't spend the next ten years paying off a credit card balance. I strongly recommend that you save up and pay cash for your next vacation. And read Rachel Cruze's book *Love Your Life Not Theirs*.

HOMEWORK

1. Think back to your last raise or tax refund. What did you do with this "found" money? Did you use some of it to increase your saving/investing? Or did you use all of it to increase your lifestyle by going out to eat more and other things you used to do more frugally?

2. Could you go back to a college lifestyle, even temporarily, to increase your saving/investing?

3. What areas of your budget have grown (beyond inflation) that are really opportunities to increase your saving/investing?

Chapter 8

LET'S PLAY OFFENSE: CAREER ADVICE

Expense management is very important, but some life **expenses** can't be avoided. Let's try something different—earn more money! See Figure 9 for a chart from Federal Reserve data. This is individual income by age and percentile in 2023.

Age	25th Percentile	50th Percentile	75th Percentile	90th Percentile
25	$25,000	$40,000	$56,662	$82,047
35	$30,026	$53,000	$85,025	$134,956
45	$32,200	$55,600	$95,001	$150,651
55	$33,000	$61,893	$101,850	$163,063
65	$35,000	$60,000	$100,280	$156,840

Figure 9: Income by Age and Percentile

If you're in the 25th or 50th percentile, then you should consider ways to increase your income. The vast majority of your income is needed to cover your basic living expenses. Having a bigger shovel makes it easier to create margin to be able to save and invest.

Ways you might increase your income:

- Ask for more hours (if you get paid overtime).

- Request a raise; gather some evidence and present a compelling case for how valuable you are to the company.

- Change companies. Many times you can expect a 10% bump for "jumping ship," but be careful, don't switch too often—no more than once every three years is my advice.

- Switch careers. See the advice later in this chapter about the StrengthsFinder 2.0 book. Find a career that takes advantage of your existing strengths and preferences.

- Go back to school and learn a new skill.

- Get a side gig. It doesn't have to be complicated. Maybe it's delivering pizzas or driving an Uber.

I have put together some advice that has served me well in my career in demonstrating my value. These tips probably line up best for office workers, but I still think they apply to most jobs. I am convinced that employers will recognize ($) valuable employees over time. Cream rises to the top!

Jimmy's Career Advice

- Be independent. A valuable employee takes initiative and runs with something but knows when to ask for help/ guidance. If you identify a problem, take ownership of it and think of solutions; don't just identify the problem.

- Stay positive. A valuable employee is cautiously optimistic even when presented with something new or difficult.

- Ask questions. Don't be afraid to ask questions about

activities that you perform or things that you don't understand.

- Question the status quo. Ask if a task can be done more accurately or efficiently from time to time—just because we have always done it that way doesn't necessarily make it the best way.

- Learn something new. Volunteer to try something that you are interested in or haven't been involved with in the past. It will broaden your scope and give you a different perspective. Most employers value well-rounded employees.

- Look forward. Find out what it takes to be at the next level. In other words, if you are a junior accountant, review the job description and ensure that you are doing your tasks well. Once you have achieved that, look at the job description for an accountant and strive to learn those tasks too.

- Be a team player. If you are caught up and see somebody who is overwhelmed, offer to help.

- Focus on the customer. Think about your internal customers and their perspectives, and seek feedback. Some specific examples: answer emails and phone calls within 24 hours, try to sync (to a certain extent) your schedule with theirs.

- Expect excellence and be flexible in order to meet customer needs / deadlines.

- Develop GRIT. GRIT is the concept that when the going gets tough, you get tougher and persevere. See Angela Lee Duckworth's video on TED TV: https://shorturl.at/

QBNdc

- <u>Improve your critical thinking skills.</u>

Grow your critical thinking skills

I read a good article in Strategic Finance magazine (yep, I'm that big of a nerd) and thought they offered some great advice on how to develop and grow your critical thinking skills. Critical thinking, IMHO, will help you in most aspects of your life, including on your personal financial journey.

Critical thinking is a manner of thinking that employs curiosity, skepticism, analysis, and logic. Why do you need strong critical thinking skills? Because you need to expand your personal accountability beyond sticking to a budget to include wealth creation (increasing your net worth!), with increasing responsibility for strategy (don't let your finances happen to you, be intentional about where you want to go—set goals!).

One of their suggestions is to focus on data analysis (use your personal financial history)—to think analytically and apply tools to help extract insights and actionable information from your history.

Evaluate your critical thinking skills

- How often do I ask insightful "why" questions?
- How frequently do I generate compelling new ideas?
- How inclined am I to challenge the validity of new information?
- How vigorously do I tackle unfamiliar, complex problems?
- How adept am I at making decisions under uncertainty?

One of the suggested critical thinking activities is to perform a SWOT (strengths, weaknesses, opportunities, and threats) analysis. I know the process is designed for business, but I think you can apply it to your personal finances too. I suggest you perform a SWOT analysis of your personal finances; maybe budgeting is a weakness for your household.

Career Management

Most **millionaire**s chose wisely in their occupation by selecting something they enjoyed and were good at. Those two things are probably related. You most likely don't enjoy doing something you aren't that good at. I strongly encourage you to get *StrengthsFinder 2.0* by Gallup and Tom Rath. This isn't a typical book; you only need to read two or three chapters (say what? [Ron Burgundy voice]). It's an unusual book because it starts by directing you to an online survey about your preferences/personality, and that survey measures your work-related strengths.

Think of it this way, if Patrick Mahomes discovers that he is a terrible tennis player (he probably isn't, but hey, work with me), should he spend a bunch of time trying to improve this shortcoming? Or would he be better off focusing on improving his extraordinary QB skills? The answer is so easy even Captain Oblivious would get this one right. The same thought process applies to your career and job choices.

Many surveys indicate that an overwhelming majority (between 70% and 80%) of Americans hate/dislike their jobs. Don't complain about it—do something about it!

Take the *StrengthsFinder* survey and figure out your top 5 strengths and which occupations are your best fit. My top strength is that I'm analytical, which fits really well in my chosen field of accounting/finance. I'm an oddball because I really like my job (most days anyhow). I'm fortunate because I am working in a field well-suited to my personal makeup. It's more than just choosing the right occupation though.

Five more career tips:

1. Take the *StrengthsFinder* survey and figure out what you're good at (see above if you skipped that part).

2. Research the industry and the company before you interview for a prospective job. Don't go in uninformed.

3. Ask candid questions of existing employees (if you can).

4. Find out about the management style of your immediate supervisor. You will be unhappy if you expect independence and end up working for a micromanager.

5. Know your worth. There are lots of ways to research online: payscale.com, salary.com, glassdoor.com. These sites can help you establish a range of what your salary should be based on your skills, experience, field, location, etc. The internet is an amazing resource—take advantage of it. The best time to negotiate your salary is before you accept the position. Go online and look for industry forums. Read industry salary guides. Do your homework and know what you are worth. Knowledge is power.

HOMEWORK

1. Purchase StrengthsFinder 2.0, take the personality / preference survey, and read the chapters that apply to your strengths and preferences.

2. How does this compare to your current job? Should you consider a different role in your company, or maybe even a different company altogether? Speak to your supervisor about what you learn about your strengths and preferences.

3. How does your income compare to the average in your field? Check salary.com, payscale.com, or glassdoor.com.

Chapter 9

4 RISKS WORTH TAKING

Should you take risks in your personal finance journey? The answer depends on your risk tolerance, but I'll list some that I took and why they made sense for me.

Jimmy's Top 4 Financial Risks

- Obtaining a college degree
- Investing in real estate
- Starting a business
- Investing in the stock market

Education can certainly be risky. It might take you four or five years to get your undergraduate degree, more if you get your master's. The cost of education can easily exceed $25,000 per year, so you could quickly spend $100,000 on a four-year degree. Investing that same $100,000 could become $7 million by age 65, assuming a 10% rate-of-return. That's a big opportunity cost. I believe your salary with a degree needs to be about $15,000 more per year versus a salary without a degree to justify going to college. Forgoing four years of salary you would've earned during your college years is a significant opportunity cost.

To add insult to injury, many are investing this $100,000 in their education using student loans. Four out of ten student loans are for folks who didn't complete their degree—yikes! Only 27% of students work in their field of study—double yikes! The average undergrad student debt is $33,500, per the Education Data Initiative. I had an accounting internship during my undergrad at UNC. This internship prepared me for what to expect from an accounting job. It helped me to not become part of the 73% of folks who no longer work in their field of study.

You need to be intentional about what you want to do with your degree. Research what a job in your field might pay once you have your degree. There are many websites, like salary.com or glassdoor.com, that will estimate what a particular job pays in your field in your region of the country.

Best undergrad college majors based on highest pay
(per CNBC and Business News Daily)
1) Petroleum engineering
2) Industrial engineering
3) Computer science
4) Interaction design
5) Public accounting

Worst undergrad majors based on lowest pay
1) Family and consumer sciences
2) General social sciences
3) Performing arts
4) Social services
5) Anthropology

I'll give a couple of tips/hacks on how to approach a traditional four-year degree.
- Consider going to a community college for the first two

years to save on tuition.

- Make sure your student loans don't exceed your first year's salary.
- Obtain a part-time job in college to help keep your student loans low.

I had a couple of part-time jobs during my college days, and it definitely helped. I graduated with $20,000 of student loans and my first year's salary was $37,500.

While I'm on the subject of education, there are many fields that don't require a college degree yet still pay a healthy salary. And there are many trade schools as well; plumbers, electricians, etc. can make serious bank.

Top paying jobs without a 4-year degree (per the BLS)

1)	Air traffic controller	$122,990
2)	Nuclear power reactor operator	$100,530
3)	Transportation/storage manager	$92,460
4)	Police supervisor	$87,910
5)	Commercial pilot	$86,080
6)	Power plant dispatcher	$85,950
7)	Radiation therapist	$85,560
8)	Elevator installer and repairer	$84,990
9)	Detective/criminal investigator	$83,170
10)	Power plant operator	$81,990

Start a business/invest in real estate

Starting your own business is hard. You need to have passion and commitment to make it work. Having said that, it's one of the most common ways millionaires have increased their net worth. Folks want the freedom to be their own boss: to control their time and work on their terms, not on the terms of a micromanaging boss.

I will start by sharing my little side gig. It's actually more my wife's business, but I like to think it's a team effort (it's not).

About twelve years ago, my wife and I started McDowell Mountain Getaway LLC. This business is a vacation rental of our log home in southern McDowell County, which is about forty-five minutes east of Asheville, in the foothills of the Blue Ridge Mountains. I love spending time in the Blue Ridge Mountains. I've always found it to be peaceful and picturesque. The food is great too; my favorite is Tupelo Honey in Asheville. From our street, you can view the Blue Ridge Mountains in the distance. Pictures just don't do it justice . . .

The heavens declare the glory of God. The expanse shows his handiwork. (Psalm 19:1)

We chose to build a log cabin because land and housing prices declined significantly following the "great" recession of 2008–2009. I don't think we would make the same decision today because labor and building materials have increased so significantly. I recall one report that indicated the cost to build a home has increased by over 90%, just since 2009 (United States Census Bureau Single-Family House Construction index), meaning our $160,000 cabin would cost over $300,000 to build today.

Another reason I have for justifying our investment is diversification. While stocks and bonds make up a big component of our retirement savings, I also believe in diversification and think real estate and other non-financial assets complement traditional retirement savings (e.g., 401(k), pension, etc.)

We market our vacation rental exclusively through Airbnb. We have been pretty happy with this arrangement. Airbnb rents our property between 100 and 120 days per year. Basically, this results in between $15,000 and $25,000 of annual revenue. It's basically cash neutral, whereby the rent pays normal operating costs. I say "normal" because we have spent some of our own money on capital projects such as adding an outdoor patio, new deck, fire pit, completing some landscaping projects, and partially finishing the basement. We selected a 10-year mortgage (to reduce the total interest expense) and hope that the rent will essentially pay the operating costs for ten years, and ultimately, we will own the property outright—essentially using other people's money.

I say it's not for everyone because my wife works really hard keeping up with renters and making sure the property is clean and presentable for our guests. It takes a lot of time, work, and patience, and negative online reviews can quickly hurt your image. We haven't had any bad reviews, but I have seen some (for other listings), and it's a little intimidating knowing we don't have any control over what people choose to say about our property and their recent stay.

My example of starting a business is really a side hustle. If you choose to start your own business and do it full time, ask yourself four questions:

1) What do you love?
2) What are you good at?
3) What does the world need?
4) What can you be paid for?

If you draw overlapping circles from these four questions, your dream job is at the center of where the circles overlap.

Maybe you have identified your dream job and want to become an entrepreneur. If so, I recommend you take a couple of steps in preparation before you leave your existing job. Save up a cash reserve of two-to-three years since most new businesses take this amount of time to become profitable. In the meantime, your bills will continue to come in each month. Put together a five-to-seven-year plan and stress-test it.

To stress-test your plan, consider three possible outcomes: 1) a dream scenario whereby it's highly profitable and you reach your goals early, 2) a middle-of-the-road scenario whereby it's not nearly as profitable and takes longer to become profitable, and 3) the "this was a tremendous mistake" scenario whereby it fails, you spend through your cash reserve, and it's still not profitable.

Hope for the best but prepare for the worst. Realize that 22% of new businesses fail in the first year, while 66% (two-thirds) fail in the first ten years (per Zippia). The average small business owner makes $62,000 per year. Consider what you are passionate about and what skills you have that the market is willing to pay for. Then make it happen!

Let's talk about the dream scenario for a rental property, using the purchase of a $500,000 house with a $100,000 down payment. Five years later, the property has appreciated to $750,000 (not hard to imagine in the current real estate market). On the surface, it appears you have realized a 50% return (woo-hoo!); but it's actually much better because your investment was only $100,000, and now you have a $250,000 gain. That's a 250% return (break out the champagne!). This example illustrates how a leveraged real estate deal can really help your net worth. But buyer beware, the dream scenario doesn't always happen. I have realized a 13.4% average annual return on my rental property due to appreciation. The property appreciated at about 5% annually, but I realized the 13.4% return via the power of leverage (i.e., using other people's money).

There are also great tax benefits to a rental business via a depreciation (tax) deduction. But this deduction gets phased out if your income exceeds a certain threshold. For most, this is an adjusted gross income (AGI) of $150,000. The point is to check with a tax professional to understand how a rental property could impact your tax situation.

A real estate investment isn't for everyone. But since most homes appreciate, at least at the rate of inflation, it's a reasonable way to diversify your retirement savings. If you invest in a real estate rental, realize that values can go down (especially over shorter periods of time), even though they tend to go up over longer periods of time. Real estate values increased 4.1% from 2000 to 2023 (Federal Reserve), a little higher than overall inflation (BLS). You will need a strong cash reserve in case you need to make repairs or renovations. You are the landlord and responsible to make necessary repairs. Plus, there are going to be times when you are in between renters.

One strategy you might consider is to hang on to your starter home rather than sell it when you choose to get a larger home. I think this is especially worth your consideration if your new home is relatively close to your old home. I believe I would be in a better financial position today if I had kept my first home, a small townhouse. I purchased it for about $100,000 in 2000, but it's worth more than $300,000 (Zillow) today. If I had rented my townhouse, rather than sell it, the price appreciation alone would have been a nice addition to my net worth. Keep in mind that if you choose to become a landlord, you'll need to find good tenants as well as maintain the house. You'll need a healthy cash reserve and more than a little patience to be a responsible landlord.

If you plan to rent your house out through Airbnb or VRBO, realize that local zoning might prohibit this; do your research ahead of time and be aware that regulations can change.

Going to college, starting a business, and investing in real estate require a tremendous amount of effort on your part; they're active, meaning they require a lot of work and sacrifice. The fourth risk, however, is passive. Passive income requires no further effort on your part past the initial investment. Some would call passive income mailbox money, because you can be lazy and only need to collect the income it generates. This makes the next investment the most attractive risk you should probably take.

Invest in the stock market

Over the past 100 years, the stock market has averaged a 10.5% rate-of-return (**S&P 500 index**), but it's not a guarantee. Some years the stock market is up, some years it's down. You have to be disciplined and stay invested (i.e., **dollar-cost averaging**, always be buying), and give your investments time to grow. Compounding can only add its magic if you sprinkle in time.

I think everyone should invest in the stock market. It's probably your best opportunity to outpace inflation, which will erode the purchasing power of your savings. Invest in the stock market for the long term, and chances are you will be amazed at how much your investments grow.

My experience has been a 6.8% rate-of-return over my twenty-five years of investing in the stock market/401(k).

But how do you invest in the stock market? If your employer offers a 401(k) or 403(b), then you have access through your employer. At least initially, keep it simple and invest in a low-cost S&P 500 index (passive) fund. Most employer plans have this option.

If you don't have access to a 401(k) or 403(b), then invest in an IRA. You can do this through a bank, but I think you're more likely to get better customer service from a financial services firm like Vanguard, Fidelity, or Charles Schwab. You can open an account with any of these financial services firms and create your own 401(k)-like plan (except there won't be any **company match**). Once you open an IRA, traditional or **Roth** (more about that in chapter 10), then select the investment you would like to participate in. I suggest you keep it simple, at least at first, and invest in a low-cost S&P 500 index. You should automate your draft through your bank or credit union and invest each month (dollar-cost average) toward a brighter future.

Invest 20% (which includes any company contributions) and don't try to time the market; time *in* the market is much more important.

Investing in stocks is just one option. We'll discuss other investing opportunities in chapter 10.

HOMEWORK

1. What risks have you taken on your journey? Have they been worth it?

2. Should you consider any additional risks? Discuss with your spouse or accountability partner.

Chapter 10

INVESTING STRATEGIES: COMPOUNDING IS THE 8TH WONDER OF THE WORLD

Hopefully in chapter 9 I convinced you that **investing** in the **stock market** is a good idea. About 40% of Americans, however, do not invest in the stock market . . .

But this isn't the only avenue to investing. Plus, there are some important guidelines I would like you to consider as you invest for the future.

Jimmy's Investing Rules

- Save early and often. The power of **compounding** enables dollars invested in your twenties to be your most powerful and effective dollars because they have the most time to compound and grow. A dollar invested at age 20 can grow to $77 by age 65. That same $1 will only become $30 if you wait to invest until age 30, using 10% returns.

- Strive to achieve a 20% savings rate. Maintain that savings rate for twenty-five to thirty years. I know 20% is aspirational in your twenties, but I want you to have options in **retirement**. If your household income is less than $200,000, include any company contributions in your 20% savings rate.

- Automate, automate, automate. Automate your monthly contributions to occur each and every month. Consistency is the name of the game.

- Diversify. Invest in stocks, **bonds**, real estate, etc.

- Watch those fees. Active mutual funds can be pretty proud with their high fees. I encourage you to select low-cost index funds instead of active mutual funds.

- Avoid 401(k) loans. Something like 18% get these types of loans (oh my). There are many risks that come with a **401(k)** loan, including tax disadvantages. There's usually a better option than a 401(k) loan.

- Stay Invested. Time in the market is more important than trying to time the market. **Dollar-cost averaging** is the way to go. Always be buying.

- Take advantage of asset location. Tax-deferred, tax "free," and after tax; I recommend all three buckets.

- Maintain momentum. The first $100,000 is the toughest, but you need to achieve escape velocity to allow compounding growth to do its work.

The first $100,000 . . .

Saving your first $100,000 is the toughest, but it's the most crucial for building wealth.

"The first $100,000 is a . . ., but you gotta do it . . . If it means walking everywhere and not eating anything that wasn't purchased with a coupon, find a way . . . " —Charlie Munger

Once you have $100,000 saved/invested, the next $100,000 will come quicker and the next $100,000 quicker still, and so on . . .

It took me about ten years to save/invest my first $100,000 (about 2000 to 2010, not a good decade for **Mr. Market**), then four more to hit $200,000, two more to hit $300,000, two more to hit $400,000, two more to hit $500,000, one more to hit $600,000, one more to hit $700,000, two more to hit $800,000, one more to hit $900,000, and finally one more to hit $1,000,000 at age 50.

Annual Savings	Years
$4,000	13.5
$5,000	11.8
$6,000	10.1
$7,000	9.0
$8,000	8.1
$9,000	7.5
$10,000	6.6
$11,000	6.1
$12,000	5.7
$13,000	5.4
$14,000	4.9
$15,000	4.5

Figure 10: Years to Hit Your First $100,000

Figure 10 assumes 8% growth.

Why 20%?

You've already heard me pound the table and recommend you save and invest 20% during your working career. Why 20%? That sounds arbitrary and capricious. I'm convinced that **saving** 20% consistently over your working career gives you the best chance to retire with dignity. Let's do some math (see Figure 11) to see what 20% does for our old friend Average Joe.

- Joe starts his working career making $56,662 at age 25.

- Joe contributes 20% of his salary (including company contributions) to his **401(k)** plan from ages 25 to 65.

- Joe gets 2% raises each year.

- When Joe retires at age 65, his salary will be $125,112.

Joe will have contributed $709,522 to his 401(k) ($1,313 per month). He'll get another $2,417,467 contribution from Mr. Market, assuming a 7% **rate-of-return** (long-term average is 10%, but let's be a little conservative), with a total retirement nest egg of $3,126,989 at age 65. It's amazing that Joe only contributed $709,522 but has a $3.1 million nest egg. Mr. Market contributed 77% of the balance. Compounding growth really is the 8th Wonder of the World! It isn't linear—it's exponential.

Age	Salary	Beg. Bal	Contributions	7% return	End Bal
25	56,662	0	11,332	397	11,729
26	57,795	11,729	11,559	821	24,109
27	58,951	24,109	11,790	1,688	37,587
28	60,130	37,587	12,026	2,631	52,244
29	61,333	52,244	12,267	3,657	68,168
30	62,559	68,168	12,512	4,772	85,451
31	63,811	85,451	12,762	5,982	104,195
32	65,087	104,195	13,017	7,294	124,506
33	66,389	124,506	13,278	8,715	146,499
34	67,716	146,499	13,543	10,255	170,297
35	69,071	170,297	13,814	11,921	196,032
36	70,452	196,032	14,090	13,722	223,845
37	71,861	223,845	14,372	15,669	253,886
38	73,298	253,886	14,660	17,772	286,318
39	74,764	286,318	14,953	20,042	321,313
40	76,260	321,313	15,252	22,492	359,057
41	77,785	359,057	15,557	25,134	399,748
42	79,340	399,748	15,868	27,982	443,599
43	80,927	443,599	16,185	31,052	490,836
44	82,546	490,836	16,509	34,359	541,704
45	84,197	541,704	16,839	37,919	596,462
46	85,881	596,462	17,176	41,752	655,391
47	87,598	655,391	17,520	45,877	718,788
48	89,350	718,788	17,870	50,315	786,973
49	91,137	786,973	18,227	55,088	860,289
50	92,960	860,289	18,592	60,220	939,101
51	94,819	939,101	18,964	65,737	1,023,802
52	96,716	1,023,802	19,343	71,666	1,114,811
53	98,650	1,114,811	19,730	78,037	1,212,578
54	100,623	1,212,578	20,125	84,880	1,317,583
55	102,635	1,317,583	20,527	92,231	1,430,341
56	104,688	1,430,341	20,938	100,124	1,551,402
57	106,782	1,551,402	21,356	108,598	1,681,356
58	108,917	1,681,356	21,783	117,695	1,820,835
59	111,096	1,820,835	22,219	127,458	1,970,513
60	113,318	1,970,513	22,664	137,936	2,131,112
61	115,584	2,131,112	23,117	149,178	2,303,407
62	117,896	2,303,407	23,579	161,238	2,488,224
63	120,254	2,488,224	24,051	174,176	2,686,451
64	122,659	2,686,451	24,532	188,052	2,899,034
65	125,112	2,899,034	25,022	202,932	3,126,989

Figure 11: Saving and Investing 20% Example

If Joe uses a **4% safe withdrawal rate (SWR)**, then he can generate a $125,080 "salary" from his nest egg ($3,126,989 X 4% SWR). This nest egg "salary" is equal to his last year's salary. His nest egg is replacing 100% of his salary! This is an oversimplified example but illustrates how saving 20% can help fund your retirement **expenses**.

Joe will probably get some benefit from **Social Security**, and his retirement expenses are likely lower (maybe 30%) than his pre-retirement expenses, so there is some "cushion" built into this oversimplified analysis. But hopefully this illustrates why saving 20% gives you some good options come quitting time.

But how/when/where should you invest that 20%?

The first step is to make sure you contribute enough to your retirement plan to get the **company match**. The company match is free money—money your employer is trying to give you. It comes with a 100% guaranteed rate-of-return!

I realize you might not be able to contribute 20% right out of the gate. I get it. Life's hard. But start somewhere, even if it's only $100 per month. Start the saving and investing habit. Grow your savings to a 20% rate over time. Remember the 20% savings rate includes both your contributions and any company contributions you receive. I also realize that in your thirties, you will be in the messy middle and might not be able to save 20% each and every year. That's OK. Keep going and get back to 20% when you can. I know this isn't going to be easy. Otherwise, everyone would be doing it. And the truth is, they're not. But you can!

The next step is to choose an investment in your 401(k) or IRA. I suggest a low-cost **S&P index fund** because an index fund has low fees. An S&P index invests in the 500 largest US companies. You're investing in the best innovation money can buy. History indicates this innovation will pay off in the long run.

Another option is to select a low-cost "lifestyle fund" (a.k.a., target maturity funds) based on the year you expect to retire. A lifestyle fund is a hybrid investment that invests in both stocks and bonds, to add **diversification**. Bonds are loans to corporations. They've historically had returns of 5%–6%, not nearly as impressive as stocks but they have less risk. Many choose to invest 80% in stocks and 20% in bonds.

A lifestyle fund does the allocation for you, including rebalancing (see below for a definition). It also shifts your portfolio to be more reliant on bonds as you approach your retirement date to minimize **sequence of return risk**. It gets more conservative the closer you get to retirement. Maybe it shifts from 80/20 to 60/40. It's most likely cheaper to invest in a low-cost S&P 500 index fund and separately into a low-cost bond fund and do the rebalancing yourself. I'd recommend annual rebalancing if you pursue a DIY approach. I think rebalancing is particularly helpful as you are about to enter retirement.

> **Rebalancing** – the periodic adjustment required to get back to a desired portfolio allocation. Say Joe wants to maintain a 60/40 portfolio of stocks and bonds. But after a significant stock market decline, his portfolio switches to 50/50. Joe would sell bonds and buy stocks to get back to his desired 60/40 portfolio allocation. Rebalancing in retirement is one way to take advantage and buy stocks when they are "on sale."

I encourage you to invest in indexes (passive) rather than actively managed mutual funds. Actively managed mutual funds charge higher fees, and only 6% of mutual funds beat the S&P return. And those 6% aren't the same funds each year. I don't think you should try to beat the market, just be the market. The long-term average return for the stock market is over 10%. I'll take a 10% return with low fees any day.

In your twenties and thirties, I'd keep it simple and invest 100% in a low-cost S&P index. In your forties, I'd start to invest some, maybe 20%, of future contributions into bonds. Note that you can increase your retirement contributions (tax deferral) once you reach age 50 through "catch-up" contributions. The IRS allows you to defer up to $30,500 once you reach the age of maturity (50), rather than $23,000 (normal limit) if you're younger than 50. In your sixties, I'd increase the bond allocation to maybe 40% (a 60/40 portfolio allocation).

You might need to extend the 80/20 allocation for longer if you're playing catch-up with your retirement contributions. **Wealth** building and wealth preservation are two different strategies. You don't need to keep scoring touchdowns after you've won the game. Don't take more risks than you need to, especially as you enter retirement. Your portfolio has less time to recover if there is a significant downturn (20% or more) as you retire.

A significant downturn in the stock market, when you first enter retirement, is called sequence of returns risk. Over 100 years, the stock market has averaged about 10% returns, but it can be much more volatile over shorter periods of time. Let's say Joe retired at the end of 2007 with a $500,000 portfolio. The bear market from 2007 to 2009 took down the value of the stock market by 50%! His portfolio would now be worth $250,000. Houston, we have a problem! It will take a 100% return on his $250,000 to get back to his original $500,000 portfolio balance, and it might take several years for that to happen. Sequence of returns risk is one of the main reasons I recommend diversification.

There are other options to help diversify (see definition below) your investments. Some encourage having 5%–10% of your retirement portfolio in cash/**money market funds**. While money market funds only earn about 4%–5% nowadays, it is essentially risk-free and is especially helpful if you can avoid selling when the market is way down. Having a healthy cash balance is also useful in retirement, to avoid selling stocks at steep losses.

> **Diversification** – spreading your investments among several
> options. The idea is that by investing in several companies or

types of investments (e.g., stocks, bonds, real estate), one can reduce risk and volatility, and achieve more steady returns over time. The concept is that if you're truly diversified, your investment returns depend on different factors. For example, if there is a recession and all your investments go down together, then you weren't diversified. Typically, stocks and bonds rely on different factors for their returns. Historically, bonds have exceeded the return of stocks during a recession; however, over longer periods of time, stocks perform better than bonds. Stocks are a good hedge against inflation while bonds are a good hedge against deflation. Other forms of diversification include gold, annuities, commodities, etc. Grandma said it best—don't put all your eggs in one basket.

You can also invest some of your 401(k) into mutual funds that focus on small and midcap companies as well as international equities. I prefer to keep the majority invested in US innovation, but you can sprinkle in other funds to increase your diversity as you see fit. I recommend investing in low-cost index funds rather than actively managed mutual funds.

Tax location

This wonky CPA topic is important, so please don't go to sleep.

Your 401(k) probably gives you the option of contributing pre-tax dollars (i.e., traditional, tax-deferred) or after-tax dollars (i.e., a **Roth**). You should consult with your CPA on your specific tax situation, but I'll provide some oversimplified guidelines that I've used.

If your marginal tax rate (the tax on the next dollar of income) is over 25% (federal and state combined), then I'd favor a traditional investment. A traditional investment is tax-deferred, meaning you get a tax deduction now but have to pay the tax later in retirement. Saving 25% or more on my tax return today is a motivating factor to go the tax-deferral route.

If your combined federal/state marginal tax rate is less than 25%, then I would encourage you to go the tax "free" route (i.e., a Roth account). With a Roth account, you don't get a tax deduction today, meaning you are contributing after-tax dollars. But your Roth investment will grow tax-free, and you'll withdraw those dollars tax-free in retirement. Roth account dollars are especially powerful, as Uncle Sam has no future claims on your money. You've already paid the tax. Because a Roth is so powerful, the government limits how much you can contribute. The limit is currently $7,500 per year. Roth contributions also have income limits. Consult with your tax preparer to ensure you qualify for a Roth contribution. For example, a single person can't contribute to a Roth if their income is greater than $161,000 (2024).

One more investing bucket I want to cover is after-tax contributions, a.k.a. a brokerage account. A brokerage account is the most flexible of the three options. Both traditional and Roth accounts can't be accessed until age 59.5, except under very limited circumstances that would likely involve penalties and fees. Some 401(k) plans have a "Rule of 55" loophole, whereby you can avoid the 10% early withdrawal penalty (sometimes as early as age 50), but check with your plan administrator on the specific limitations and rules of your plan.

A brokerage account can be accessed any time, but there aren't any tax advantages like there are with a Roth or traditional IRA. The 59.5 rule doesn't apply to brokerage contributions. You should probably contribute to a brokerage account after you've maxed out the first two tax-advantaged buckets. A brokerage account is especially attractive to those who want to retire early. We'll discuss the **FIRE movement** more in chapter 14.

Final thoughts

Avoid 401(k) loans. These loans take your investments out of the market and have tax disadvantages. I'd limit 401(k) loans to a last resort. If the bank is about to foreclose on your house, then a 401(k) loan might be your best bad option. It is also slightly less bad than a hardship withdrawal.

Some folks like to invest in individual stocks, especially in a brokerage account. I'd say this is a bad idea for most folks. If you choose to invest in individual stocks, please limit this to no more than 10% of your portfolio. If professional money managers can't consistently beat their index benchmark, then you probably can't either. However, if you do your homework and want to invest a small portion into individual stocks, then have at it, but realize this is not a passive way to invest. You'll need to listen to quarterly earnings calls and really understand the industry, and the risks and opportunities that lie ahead. Stick to your circle of competence.

Investing in stocks, bonds, and real estate involves patience and perseverance. The stock market will go down periodically, but over time, it will continue to go up. The old stock market cliché is to buy low and sell high. This seems obvious, but the emotional side of you may try to do the opposite. Stay the course. Buying low means buying stocks when they are going down (look out below!) and selling stocks when everyone likes them. Your best bet during a period of stock losses is to buy more. Stocks are on sale when they lose value. Dollar-cost averaging is the way to go. Always be buying.

If the stock market goes down 20%, don't think you need to take action. Don't just do something, stand there. Buy and hold (through thick and thin) is my philosophy. Don't trade frequently, especially in your 401(k). Over time, the stock market is likely to recover and go higher still. At least that's what history indicates. If you try to time the market, you have to be right twice, when you expect the market to go down, and again right before the market goes back up. That's a fool's errand.

Putnam Investments did a study showing the total market return over a fifteen-year period. It was 10.66%. However, if you missed the ten best days of this fifteen-year period, your return dropped to 5%. If you missed the thirty best days over a fifteen-year period, your return was actually *negative* 1.2%. This illustrates that trying to time the market is a futile mission. Nobody knows when these thirty best days are going to occur, not even the geniuses on Wall Street.

Successful investing takes hard work, discipline, perseverance, and time. The size of your portfolio is determined by your savings rate, your return, and time. The only one of these three you truly control is your savings rate.

My investing strategy doesn't rely on picking the right stocks or avoiding the next recession. It relies on a high savings rate, patience (i.e., time), and optimism that the stock market will continue its upward trend. One of the reasons for my optimism is that history indicates I should be optimistic, and because innovation will continue. Artificial intelligence and machine learning are just the latest advancements to improve efficiency and increase growth.

Investing isn't a sacrifice, it's an opportunity.

HOMEWORK

1. What's your saving/investing percentage? Include any company match you get.

2. If it's less than 20%, use some critical thinking to brainstorm ways you could increase your percentage over time. Could you earn more money? Do you need to get a little more frugal with your housing, transportation, or food budgets?

3. What expenses/fees are you paying on your investments? The prospectus of your investment (e.g., mutual fund/index) will detail how much you're paying. A good, low-cost index fund charges 0.2% or less.

4. What is your investing allocation in stocks, bonds, real estate, and cash/money market? Are you diversified? I recommend an 80% stock allocation prior to age 65, transitioning to 50 or 60% in retirement.

5. What is your investing location? Do you have tax-deferred (e.g., 401(k)), tax "free" (e.g., Roth), and after-tax (e.g., brokerage account) investments? Tax diversity is advantageous in retirement, giving you options and flexibility.

SECTION II

INTERMEDIATE PERSONAL FINANCE TOPICS

Chapter 11

ARE YOU STEALING FROM THE FUTURE?

Rather than thinking about **expenses** in terms of money, I want you to consider expenses in terms of your time. Calculate how much money you make per hour; then consider how much of your time is being spent to acquire your next purchase. You aren't spending your money, you're spending your time! Think about that new iPhone you really want. You know, the one with all the latest features that everyone else will have. Take that $1,000 price tag and divide it by your hourly wage and consider how much time you are really paying for the latest gadget. Is it really worth that much of your time? Don't forget that time is finite (*it's not renewable*); try as you may, you can't create more time. Once you use it—it's gone!

Let's say you do the math and determine it's still worth it. Now consider the **opportunity cost**—the forgone value of an alternative (#FOMO). What are you giving up by spending the money now? What is the cost of missing out on an alternative use of this money?

Here's an example to illustrate the opportunity cost concept. Let's stick with the $1,000 iPhone (might be more than a week's worth of your wages). That same $1,000 could be used, instead, to invest in your

retirement; that's the alternative in this example. That same $1,000 will become almost $16,000 in thirty years (10% compounded annually). So, the opportunity cost of choosing to spend $1,000 now is short-changing your retirement by about $16,000. *Are you stealing from the future?* Your future. Are your purchasing decisions today delaying your **financial independence** day?

I'm not saying you shouldn't spend money, but I do want you to consider the consequences of your purchasing decisions. I believe you should ask some hard questions before you buy:

- Can I really afford this? Does it fit in my monthly **budget** without debt?

- Is it a good value? Remember, price is what you pay, value is what you get. Do some research online and compare this item to its competitors; maybe there's an alternative (used maybe) that costs less? If you find a lower priced alternative, maybe it's almost as good as the more expensive option. My oversimplified philosophy is to avoid the cheapest and the most expensive, favoring something in the middle.

- Is this item really going to make me happier two weeks from now?

- Does this help or hurt my goal of financial independence?

- Do I want to look rich or be rich? You probably can't do both.

- Is it really worth the time I am going to have to work to earn it?

- How long would I have to save to pay cash? If it's truly a priority, then make the effort to set aside enough money up-front.

HOMEWORK

1. Do you consider how many hours or life energy it takes to make purchases?

2. Do you have a framework/method to evaluate purchases (similar to the seven points in this chapter)?

3. Consider the opportunity cost of your next big purchase. In other words, what could that same amount of money grow to by age 65 if you invest it instead?

4. Are you saving more for tomorrow or paying more for the past? Compare your monthly debt payments to your monthly retirement contributions.

Chapter 12

SOCIAL SECURITY: WILL IT REALLY HELP YOU IN RETIREMENT?

A: Most likely

Many believe that **Social Security** is a **retirement** benefit that is going bankrupt and simply won't be there by the time they need it. Twenty-five percent of people surveyed (2022 Harris Poll survey) expect to receive *no benefits* from Social Security. Social Security—both a tax and a benefit—is something of an enigma, so I decided to dedicate a chapter to better understanding this oddity, started by Franklin Roosevelt in 1935.

The tax piece

Most people reading this are probably still in their working years and have yet to realize any benefits from this safety net for seasoned citizens.

Social Security taxes apply to the first $168,600 of your income (2024). The tax rate is a flat 6.2% of your pay, up to a maximum withholding of $10,453 per year. That's referred to as the employee portion. If you have an employer (self-employed pay the full 12.4%), then your employer pays *another* 6.2% in addition to your contribution. Many analysts say that you are effectively paying both pieces (employer and employee) because your paycheck would be that much higher were it not for this "tax." I am encouraging you to understand this "tax" because it could effectively reduce your salary by up to $20,906 per year—that maximum amount applies to those fortunate enough to be in the top 5% or so of earners.

The benefits

If you've worked for at least ten years, you should be eligible for monthly benefits in retirement. The average benefit in 2023 was $1,830 per month. The more income you earn (over a thirty-five-year period), the bigger your benefit in retirement; full retirement is at age 67. You can receive 70% of your full benefit starting at age 62, and you can increase that benefit by about 8% per year by deferring when you elect to receive benefits, but you can't defer past age 70.

The benefit formula/calculation can be fairly complex and can vary based on your individual work history. There are numerous options and strategies that can be used to maximize your lifetime benefit. I'm not going to cover strategies or options, other than to state that it's essentially means-tested/regressive in the following three sharply graduated brackets:

1. 90% replacement of eligible income up to about $14,100 annually

2. 32% replacement of eligible income up to about $85,000 annually

3. 15% replacement of remaining eligible income up to the maximum/ceiling

In 2024, the maximum monthly benefit was $4,873 (at full retirement age). For very low-income seniors, Social Security replaces up to 90% of eligible earnings. For more average seniors, it is more likely to replace approximately 40% of eligible earnings (pre-retirement wages). If you are a "high" earner, you will see about a 28% replacement percentage.

Up to 85% of Social Security benefits can be subject to income tax if your combined income, including income from other sources such as part-time work, **pension, 401(k)** distributions, etc. exceed $34,000 for individuals and $44,000 for married couples. Up to 50% is taxable if your individual income exceeds $25,000 or a married couple's income exceeds $32,000. These thresholds are not adjusted for inflation, so this will "capture" more and more income over time. The math behind the combined income calculation is a little complex. Essentially, it includes 50% of your Social Security benefit in addition to your other sources of income.

Some projections indicate future funding problems with Social Security, with the program only being able to pay about 77% of promised benefits, beginning as early as 2033. I believe, through congressional action (I know that's an oxymoron, but work with me), that some additional steps will be taken (e.g., increasing payroll taxes) to make sure the program continues. It's simply too popular (about 66 million retired workers as of 2022) not to continue.

ssa.gov includes some really helpful reports, specific to you. I strongly recommend you go there and create your own account.

Benefits to setting up an account with ssa.gov

- You can review your earnings history, both for informational purposes and accuracy.

- You can find out your projected benefits in both today's dollars and in future dollars (adjusted for inflation). I prefer the future dollars calculator for retirement planning purposes.

- Using your earnings history, you can recalculate your Social Security benefit. I'll provide an example below. One of the reasons to recalculate your Social Security benefit is to better understand how much your benefit will increase if you work another couple of years. Once you have thirty-five years of earnings history, working another couple of years isn't likely to increase your benefit much.

Let's do a simplified illustration (see Figure 12) of how ssa.gov calculates your benefit:

The first step is to view your earnings history on ssa.gov. Next, get the indexing factors for your retirement, specific to when you are eligible for benefits at age 62. For me, that means 2036.

How SSA.gov Calculates Your Benefit				
	3,500,000	Total Earnings over 35 Years, Indexed for Inflation		
	100,000	Annual Earnings		
	8,333	AIME, Average Indexed Monthly Earnings		
Frst Bend	1,174	$1,057		90% Replacement
Second Bend	7,078	$2,265		32% Replacement
Third Bend	81	$12		15% Replacement
	8,333	$3,334	PIA	Estimated Benefit at Age 67

Figure 12: Social Security Benefit Example

In this example, $3,500,000 is the total of the highest thirty-five years of earnings, adjusted/indexed for inflation (using factors provided by ssa.gov). Divide this by 35 to get the average annual earnings of $100,000. Divide the annual by 12 to get the average indexed monthly earnings of $8,333. Using the bend points, the Social Security administration calculates your estimated benefit (i.e., primary insured amount [PIA]) at $3,334 per month at your full retirement age (FRA) at age 67.

Note that your Medicare premiums get deducted from your Social Security benefit check each month.

To navigate to the future dollars calculator, log into your account. Go to the bottom portion on the landing page and click on the "learn more about retirement estimates" option. Then select the "before you decide to retire" link. This will bring up a pop-up menu. Select the "benefit calculator" link in blue at the bottom, then the "online calculator" option, and then the "future (inflated) dollars" option. Enter your information, including your desired retirement date and earnings history. Hit the "calculate benefit" button near the bottom of the calculator. This is your estimated monthly benefit, in future dollars, at age 62. Increase this amount by 8% for every year you delay retirement, up to age 70.

In the online calculator, type "indexing factors" in the search bar on the upper right. Select "indexing factors for earnings" at the top of the search results. Select the year you will turn age 62, and then "submit request." This will give you the indexing factors for earnings needed to index your earnings for inflation. For example, I earned $4,110 dollars in 1990. But I need to adjust that for inflation. The ssa.gov inflation factor for 1990 is 4.8. $4,110 X 4.8 = $19,728, which is the inflation-adjusted earnings.

HOMEWORK

1. Setup a secure account with ssa.gov.

2. Review your earnings history for accuracy. Enter your earnings history into an Excel spreadsheet for analysis.

3. Extra credit: Calculate your average indexed monthly earnings and primary insured amount to see if you can match the ssa.gov estimate of your future monthly benefit.

Chapter 13

IS DEBT REALLY THAT BAD?

A: It might be . . .

There are lots of opinions about debt. Some think it's a great way to borrow your way to becoming rich (Robert Kiyosaki, author of *Rich Dad Poor Dad*, has acknowledged he has over $1.2 billion in debt), and some are super-negative about it (Dave Ramsey). I'm pretty much in the Dave Ramsey camp, but maybe we should back up and take a fresh look because I think it's a good question.

Q: Is there such a thing as *good* debt?

A: I think that's actually the wrong question.

Debt, by itself, isn't good or bad—it's not even human . . . Let's back up even further and see what the Bible has to say about debt since good and bad are spiritual concepts.

I am not a Bible scholar, but I have read the entire Bible and I don't believe it explicitly forbids debt; therefore, I don't think it's inherently wrong/sinful to have debt. However, the Bible does have a lot to say about debt. Specifically, the Bible warns against going into debt and has some pretty harsh words for those who borrow and don't pay back.

The rich rule over the poor. The borrower is servant to the lender. (Proverbs 22:7)

The wicked borrow, and don't pay back, but the righteous give generously. (Psalm 37:21)

Q: Is it a smart idea to go into debt?

A: Probably not.

Let's start specifically with an example of when I think debt is an especially bad idea. I do not recommend going into debt for a depreciating **asset**. Chapter 6 discusses transportation **expenses**/strategy. I think mathematically, transportation debt (e.g., car loans) inherently decreases your **net worth**—that's bad.

I think it's also a bad idea to cosign for someone else's debt. Cosigning (or surety) is a formal commitment to guarantee someone else's debt. Essentially, you are going into debt with (and for) someone else—someone the bank considers to be a risky investment (otherwise they wouldn't need someone to cosign). You're probably not smarter than the bank.

Q: Is there ever a situation when it is "acceptable" to go into debt?

A: Maybe.

I will start with an example. I would prefer that everyone save up and pay cash for a house—*but that's probably not realistic*. I am personally comfortable with a 15-year mortgage, especially if someone has a reasonable down payment. Why? Because houses tend to appreciate, at least at the rate of inflation, and because housing is something everyone **needs**. Plus, you can save a tremendous amount of interest on a 15-year mortgage versus a traditional 30-year mortgage. Additionally, there is a significant tax advantage (if you itemize) to purchasing a home versus renting. I believe purchasing a home is a better "deal" as long as you plan to live in your house for at least five years; otherwise, you are probably better off renting (see chapter 5). Many will argue that a 30-year mortgage gives you more flexibility, and that's true. I can support a 30-year mortgage, but make sure you have a plan to pay it off before you retire.

Now that we have established what is a *really bad* idea—going into debt for depreciating assets or guaranteeing another's debt—and an acceptable situation, a 15-year mortgage for a house . . . what about going into debt as an "investment"?

After all, I believe this is essentially Robert Kiyosaki's advice—use debt to buy investment real estate and get rich. Mathematically, I won't argue with the power of leverage; certainly some businesses (as well as individuals) have made this wager and consequently made a handsome profit in the process. Some rich people, the argument goes, have made this strategy work; therefore, you can too. I will concede that some have made it big as a result of leveraging debt. But just because someone else did it doesn't make it a smart, or even moral, strategy for all to follow.

Mr. Kiyosaki advocates using this leverage model in real estate. I presume the fallback position, if the real estate market turns south, you can always declare bankruptcy, leaving the lender on the hook. That may be legal, but I would argue it's clearly wrong not to pay back your debts. The Bible is pretty clear about that.

Having said that, the risk is just too high for me to recommend this strategy. I would rather you pay off your existing debts, starting with consumer debt first (e.g., **credit cards**) and mortgage debt last (typically appreciating assets). I'm not afraid of money, but I think a healthy level of respect for debt is warranted (common sense in my book).

At least think about it . . .

Endless cycle of debt?

Sixty-eight percent of Americans in debt doubt they'll ever pay it off, according to a recent CreditCards.com report. That's an alarming statistic and a really pessimistic view on life. I'm not denying there are real challenges that can lead to debt: medical bills, student loans, unemployment, etc. These are real issues and real problems. My trite observations won't magically fix all of these societal deficiencies; however,

I don't want this mindset to become an excuse—a reason for putting off the necessary and pragmatic steps that you can take to become (and stay) debt-free.

I believe the debt mindset is an excuse (for some) to spend beyond their means, because debt is a fait accompli, an unavoidable circumstance. If you accept that something is unavoidable, then you don't have to do anything about it—just sing kumbaya around a campfire and roast some marshmallows while you're at it.

A permanent debt cycle is not something you should merely accept as part of your life. Permanent fixtures in your life should be faith, family, and friends, not debt.

Having said that, many people reading this will say my previous rant was nice and all, but also irrelevant—they can't change the past, they already have debt! Chances are, that describes most of you. So what now? Even if we accept the premise that debt is unavoidable (a debatable, but moot point for most), what's the "procedure" if we have already become a victim of the debt monster?

Let's tackle this quandary in two stages: 8 causes of debt (hey—some younger readers might have thus far managed to avoid the debt star), and 8 steps to help reduce/eliminate debt (if you already have it).

8 common causes of debt (per Bankrate.com)

1. <u>Keeping up with the Joneses</u> – chasing a lifestyle you can't afford.

2. <u>Medical expenses</u> – lack of or lapse in health insurance are leading causes, along with chronic conditions.

3. <u>Unexpected emergency</u> – not having a sufficient **emergency fund**.

4. <u>Gambling</u> – as many as four million Americans have an addiction.

5. Loss of (primary source of) income/same expenses – could be due to being laid off, fired, or significant decline in business revenue.

6. Student loans – with the rising costs of education, this is a common cause.

7. Being poorly insured – insurance might seem like a waste of money, until you need it.

8. Divorce – can be financially devastating for both parties.

Let's dig into these pitfalls a bit deeper and explore strategies for avoiding—and dealing with—these issues (after your debt affliction).

1. Budget. Be able to quickly adapt your expenses to your lifestyle (don't overspend). Set and monitor your **budget** with a finance app (e.g., EveryDollar). Start with the heavy hitters: housing, transportation, and food (these three probably make up two-thirds of your budget). Having an emergency fund also really helps should you experience an unexpected expense. Sometimes expense mitigation isn't the only solution; you might also need to take a second/part-time job to increase the income side of the equation. If your household income is less than $50,000, I would submit that expense management might not be the only/best way to balance the budget.

2. Medical insurance. I strongly recommend that you consistently carry health insurance. Don't let it lapse— even if you have to take out a COBRA/continuation policy. You should also shop on healthcare.gov. If you already have medical debt, work with the provider to set up a reasonable short-term-arrangement (overcommunicate if necessary; don't be an optimistic

procrastinator—it won't go away on its own). Work a part-time job, if necessary, to pay off this debt as soon as possible. Review the charges and make sure they are reasonable and customary. I know it's time-consuming, but hospital billing errors are more common than you might think. I also recommend you contribute to a health savings account to have a medical emergency fund.

3. <u>$1,000 emergency fund.</u> This is your first financial priority if you don't already have an emergency fund. Save $100 per paycheck (if that's all you can do). Prioritize getting a $1,000 starter emergency fund, then build up to a three-to-six month emergency fund (of basic living expenses). Three months might be fully funded if you have a two-income household with relatively risk-free jobs. I recommend closer to six months if you're a one-income household or your job(s) are less stable.

4. <u>A gambling addiction</u> is treatable through counseling and medication. You might also seek out an accountability partner.

5. <u>Loss of income.</u> I can't answer this quickly and definitively for everyone. You might need to go back to school and get a different degree. You might have to move or commute to a better job location. Read *StrengthsFinder 2.0* to get suggestions on occupations you're best suited for. See chapter 8 on increasing your income and chapter 25 on how to prepare for a possible job loss.

6. <u>Student loans.</u> This is a sticky wicket—or a hot mess (if you are in the South like me). There are ways to avoid student loans: scholarships, community college (at least for the first two years), in-state tuition, part-time

job during school, military service before college, and trade schools. At least think about it. If you already have student loans, refinance to a lower interest rate (if available). Work a part-time job and pay it off as quickly as possible. Get Fannie Mae out of your life!

7. <u>Insurance.</u> You need to have the right insurance in place for you and your family, or a financial disaster might find you. See chapter 17 for suggested policies you need.

8. <u>Divorce.</u> The best answer for divorce is to attend counseling before you marry, and then again if you hit a rocky patch. If you have already experienced divorce, then it will take some time to rebuild your life, including your finances. See also answer to #1.

To be honest, being successful in personal finance is a whole lot more than just a math problem; it's a motivation problem. You have to really want to get out of debt. It's going to take hard work and sacrifice. I don't want you to rationalize debt just because most of your friends have debt. Staying in debt isn't the smart thing to do. Be different. Be weird. Be debt-free. Think about all the things you could do with the money you are currently spending on debt—go ahead, dream a little—now go out and make it happen!

Set some goals to get out of debt, goals that are:

Specific

Measurable

Achievable

Relevant

Time-Bound

This is Sparta! I know its random, but I needed some motivation.

Final thoughts

I will concede that debt might be necessary to get a reliable form of transportation (see also chapter 6 on how to purchase a car), and a mortgage is probably necessary to purchase a home (see also chapter 5 on how to purchase your house). However, I very much think you should pay off debt sooner rather than later and would not consider you **financially independent** until you pay off all your debts. Make sure you have a plan to get out of debt.

HOMEWORK

1. Do you have any consumer- or transportation-related debt? What's your plan to pay it off?

2. Do you have a mortgage on your home? What's your plan to pay off the mortgage? Will it be paid off by the time you retire? Is there anything you can/should do in your budget to accelerate being totally debt-free sooner?

3. How much interest did you pay last year? Check year-end bank statements and add up all the interest you paid for car loans, credit cards, student loans, and your mortgage. Imagine what you could do with the amount of interest you paid for the whole year.

If you're interested in learning more about the FIRE movement, I suggest watching the documentary *Playing with FIRE*, available on iTunes. This documentary includes interviews with Vicki Robin and Pete Adeney (a.k.a. Mr. Money Mustache).

There are also several other bloggers/websites you might want to research, including: madfientist.com, millennial-revolution.com, JL Collins (JLCollinsnh.com), or ficalc.app.

HOMEWORK

1. Do you agree or disagree with the FIRE movement principles and methods? Which ones and why?

2. Should you consider pursuing one of the flavors of FIRE?

Chapter 14

THE FIRE MOVEMENT: WHAT IS IT AND WHAT DO ITS FOLLOWERS BELIEVE?

Financial Independence, Retire Early (**FIRE**) is a movement with the goal of gaining **financial independence** and retiring at a younger than traditional age. Those seeking to join the movement proactively maximize their **saving**s rate by increasing their income and/or decreasing their **expenses**.

The idea is to accumulate investment **assets**, typically through index funds and/or rental real estate, sufficient to fund their lifestyle via a **4% safe withdrawal rate (SWR)**. The Rule of 25 entails saving and **investing** to achieve a nest egg equal to 25 times your annual expenses. When your investment income (the 4% SWR) is greater than your monthly expenses, you have reached financial independence.

A wall chart is a helpful way to track your efforts to increase income and decrease expenses over time. Include a third line to show the amount of income the 4% SWR would generate (portfolio or monthly investment). When the monthly investment income line crosses the expense line, then financial independence is achieved. This is called the crossover point (see Figure 13).

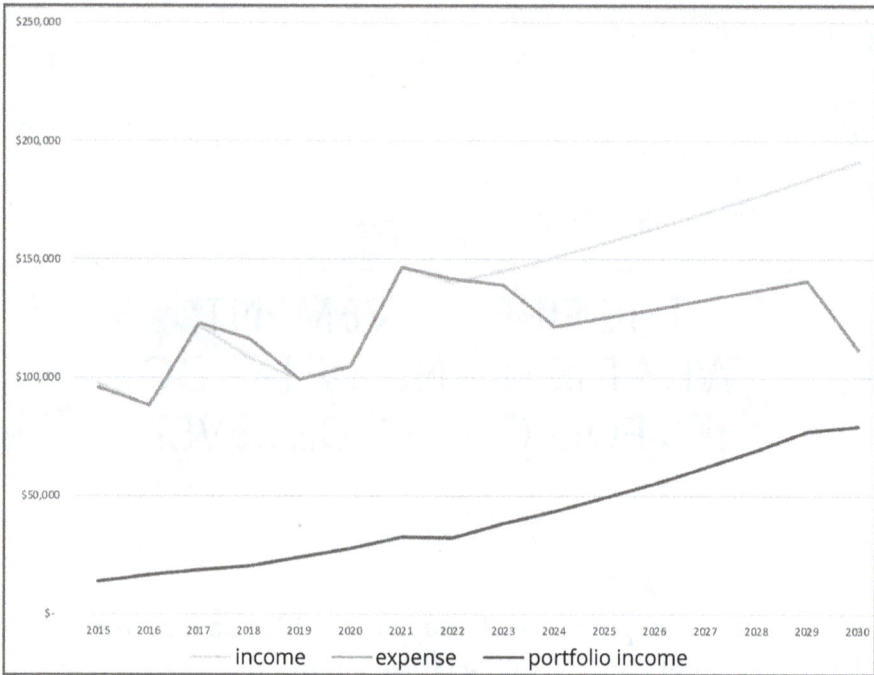

Figure 13: Financial Independence Crossover Point

Upon reaching financial independence, paid work becomes optional. Almost always, financial independence also involves being debt-free.

The **FIRE movement** got its start in the 1992 bestselling book *Your Money or Your Life* by Vicki Robin and Joe Dominguez. The *Mr. Money Mustache* blog started in 2011 and made the movement much more popular, propelled by his post, "The Shockingly Simple Math Behind Early **Retirement**." In this blog post, he illustrates the mathematical relationship between your savings rate and the time it takes to reach financial independence. For example, his chart shows that you could retire in 22 years if you have a 40% savings rate, or 17 years with a 50% savings rate.

Decreasing your expenses is deemed more powerful than increasing your income since expenses are after tax while income is before; but many pursue both. You might need $1.33 more dollars (of income) to fund a $1.00 increase in your expenses. So reducing your expenses by $1.00 is the same as increasing your income by $1.33. A penny saved is better than a penny earned . . .

Another aspect of many FIRE advocates is their commitment to DIY home/auto repairs and maintenance. The math is pretty compelling. Say you make $25 an hour and need to repair your toilet. You could hire a plumber, at maybe $150 an hour. Or you could watch a YouTube video and do the repair yourself. In essence, you're paying yourself $150 an hour to do-it-yourself.

Investment location is also important. Traditional **retirement accounts: 401(k)**, IRA, and **Roth**, all require you to be 59.5 before you begin withdrawals. There are a few exceptions to the 59.5 rule, but they frequently involve fees and penalties, or are for specific purposes (e.g., purchasing your first home). Therefore, FIRE folks put most of their investments in after-tax brokerage accounts, which can be accessed anytime. Some call this account a **bridge account**. It bridges the time in their forties and fifties (some retire in their thirties) to age 59.5, when they are able to access their traditional retirement accounts.

The several flavors of the FIRE movement

"Lean FIRE" is probably the most traditional path to financial freedom generally thought of when folks think of the FIRE movement. Lean FIRE followers are especially **frugal** and spend less than the average American. Many espouse extremely low housing and transportation costs by **house hacking** and biking to work. Some have defined this threshold at $40,000 or less. If you need $40,000 in income, then your financial independence (FI) number is $1 million ($1 million times 4% SWR = $40,000), meaning once you reach $1 million in savings, then paid work becomes optional because you can use your portfolio and a 4% SWR rate to perpetually fund your living expenses. If you need

$20,000 in income, then your FI number is $500,000. There are many popular FI bloggers who live on around $20,000 per year.

"Fat FIRE" is a version of FIRE that is generally defined by those desiring a $100,000 or more income at FI. At $100,000, you would need a nest egg of $2.5 million.

"Coast FIRE" is a version of FIRE whereby one saves aggressively, especially in their twenties and thirties, and then takes a break and lets their investments grow over time without additional aggressive savings. At this point, one might focus on passion projects and not aggressively pursue higher-income jobs.

"Barista FIRE" is a version of FIRE where one seeks to achieve a version of FI that also entails working part-time rather than outright retirement post FI. Some call this Financially Independent, Recreationally Employed. The term barista refers to working part-time at a coffee shop, but being a barista isn't really required; any part-time, low-stress job fits the description. The idea is your nest egg doesn't have to cover all your expenses, as you plan to work part-time after retiring from a full-time occupation. Since your nest egg doesn't need to be as large, you can retire to a part-time gig earlier.

Some have described the FIRE movement as a little over-the-top in their aggressive savings rates and overly frugal lifestyle. Many aggressive FIRE adherents seek to retire in their thirties, which probably means a savings rate of 50% or 60% (or more). Some observe that the required effort to achieve this rate of savings sacrifices too much of living your best life today. I'll admit that Lean FIRE isn't my cup of tea. I'm probably more in the Fat or Barista FIRE camp. I'm trying to achieve FI in my mid-fifties. While this still qualifies as retiring early (prior to age 65), I'm more comfortable saving 20%–30% and trying to achieve something akin to balance—living some today while also saving for a great, big, beautiful tomorrow.

If you're interested in learning more about the FIRE movement, I suggest watching the documentary *Playing with FIRE*, available on iTunes. This documentary includes interviews with Vicki Robin and Pete Adeney (a.k.a. Mr. Money Mustache).

There are also several other bloggers/websites you might want to research, including: madfientist.com, millennial-revolution.com, JL Collins (JLCollinsnh.com), or ficalc.app.

HOMEWORK

1. Do you agree or disagree with the FIRE movement principles and methods? Which ones and why?

2. Should you consider pursuing one of the flavors of FIRE?

Chapter 15

TOP LESSONS LEARNED FROM MILLIONAIRES

If I'm going on a trip, I like to talk to people who have been to my destination before. They're subject matter experts.

What are the most common characteristics of the **millionaire** next door? How did they achieve millionaire status? Did they get a big inheritance? Take lots of risks? How long did it take them to get there? What behaviors and beliefs guided them along their journey?

There are 11.6 million millionaire households in the United States as of 2020 (per Statista), or about 9% of all households. Let's see if we can learn from them.

Millionaires are disciplined, exhibit perseverance, have integrity, work hard, and credit choosing wisely in relation to their spouse as key factors in their success.

Thomas J. Stanley's *The Next Millionaire Next Door* (the follow-up book to the original *The Millionaire Next Door*), Ramsey Solutions, and a *Money Guy* podcast start to paint a picture of who millionaires are, and more importantly, if their approach might be helpful on your journey toward **financial independence**.

Millionaire stats:

- 85% are married, versus 50% of the general public. Note that, on average, 77% of **net worth** decreases following a divorce. (*The Money Guy Show*)

- They are in their sixties (on average), having first reached 7-figure status at age 49, after twenty-eight years of **saving** and **investing**. (Ramsey)

- Only 31% averaged more than $100,000 annually over their career. (Ramsey)

- 93% have a college degree, and nearly 60% have a graduate degree as well. (Stanley)

- More than half went to a public university, and 80% went to public K–12. (*The Money Guy Show*)

- ~80% are self-made, meaning they started with zero and didn't receive any inheritance. The corollary to this stat is that the kids and grandkids are going to spend all their **wealth**. . . (Ramsey)

- They are **frugal** and intentionally **budget**; 70% know specifically how much they spend on their living **expenses**, and more than 60% consider frugality as a critical factor in their success. 70% said their parents were frugal. (Stanley)

- They tend to drive Toyotas, Hondas, or Fords. On average, their most recent car purchase was $35,000. 64% buy cars with cash. 87% keep cars at least seven years. (Stanley)

- 72% work in their field of study versus 73% of the public that does not work in their field of study. (*The Money Guy Show*)

- 84% are optimists, versus 47% of the general public. (*The Money Guy Show*)

- 70% exercise at least three times per week. Only 15% don't exercise at all. (*The Money Guy Show*)

- 20% are retired; the 80% that are not retired work an average of 45 hours per week and get about 7.6 hours of sleep per night. (Stanley)

- 81% put less than 20% down on their first home purchase. (*The Money Guy Show*)

- 71% made personal finance a priority before age 35. (*The Money Guy Show*)

- Most have a good relationship with debt. 99% use **credit cards**, but only 3% carry a balance from month to month. (*The Money Guy Show*)

- 42% had student loans. Interesting that student loans are not a deal-breaker for 7-figure success. (*The Money Guy Show*)

- 87% have at least four months of emergency cash reserves. (*The Money Guy Show*)

- 83% save/invest at least 20%. (*The Money Guy Show*)

- 69% are savers/investors, 16% senior executives, 7% entrepreneurs, and 7% virtuosos (famous athletes, actors, etc.) (*The Money Guy Show*)

Following are some notable facts from *The Millionaire Next Door*:

- <u>Most millionaires do not live in fancy houses or drive luxury automobiles.</u> They typically live in middle-class neighborhoods and drive nondescript automobiles (i.e., not a foreign luxury car). They live well below their means and are generally frugal.

- They intentionally set out to become financially independent. They have a budget and track how well they do against that budget. They have goals: monthly, annually, and even longer. They spend a disproportionate amount of time planning their financial future.

- They strategize to minimize their taxes. Tax planning pays dividends.

- They are disproportionately entrepreneurs and self-employed. They believe being an employee is risky—you only have one source of income. This thinking is consistent with their lifestyle, which is counter to conventional wisdom and counter to conspicuous consumption habits.

- They take risks and are aware of opportunities when they see them. They enjoy what they do and chose wisely in regard to their occupation.

- Some are good at offense (generating income) and others at defense (expense management), but many are good at both.

- They are compulsive savers and investors. On average, they invest 20% of household income.

- 80% of millionaires are first-generation rich. They didn't inherit their wealth.

- Becoming a millionaire takes discipline, sacrifice, and hard work. Are the trade-offs worth the cost?

"Building wealth requires a combination of our ability and willingness to live below our means." — Sarah Stanley Fallaw, co-author of *The Next Millionaire Next Door*

HOMEWORK

What traits of millionaires do you want to emulate? Why?

Chapter 16

TAX STRATEGIES

I know this is a boring topic—I hear ya—but drink a little coffee and let's contemplate this exciting and esoteric issue—okay, okay, not so much . . . but it's important all-the-same.

One of the traits that **millionaire**s have in common is that they strategize to minimize their taxes (Thomas J. Stanley, *The Millionaire Next Door*).

How do they do it? I'll give you a hint. It's not an ancient Chinese secret. The key is to plan early in the year and set up your income and **expenses** to take advantage (legally of course) of existing tax laws.

If you go to an experienced tax planner (I prefer a CPA, but I'm inherently biased) after the fact—he or she can only keep you out of jail—that's it; CPAs are good and all, but they can't change the past. If, instead, you go to a tax planner *before the fact*, he or she can help you set up your affairs in such a way as to minimize your taxes in the coming year, as well as going forward.

This chapter couldn't possibly address each person's individual situation, so I strongly encourage you to reach out to your tax preparer/planner (get a second opinion even if you do your own taxes). Have a face-to-face meeting with your tax planner to discuss what you should be doing, going forward, to minimize your taxes (plan . . . plan . . . and then plan some more). Think of it this way, *you pay a lot in taxes every year!* Pay as little tax as you legally can. Don't make a donation to the IRS. Pick a different charity.

The most common taxes I bet you're paying:

1) Income taxes – federal and state
2) Payroll taxes – **Social Security**, Medicare, etc.
3) Property taxes on real estate
4) Gasoline/road taxes
5) Vehicle registration and property taxes
6) Sales taxes – state and municipal
7) Miscellaneous – cell phone bill, utility bills, etc.

I encourage you to calculate your total tax payments (at least once a year), and how much tax, as a percentage of your income, you pay. I believe my effective tax rate is about 30% (when I consider all taxes); that's *more than my housing expense—say what?!*

I know many of you will say there isn't much you can do about some of these taxes, especially the usage taxes (like road taxes)—maybe so—but if you are aware of how much in taxes you pay each year, you can do some strategic planning to minimize each of these taxes and consider alternative ways that might *reduce* your taxes in the future. For example, you could get a more fuel-efficient vehicle, thereby paying less in road taxes.

At the risk of sounding preachy, let me ask you to consider the following three tax reduction ideas to get your brainstorming started:

1. Contribute more to your 401(k). This tried-and-true method reduces your taxable income and helps build up your nest egg for **retirement**.

2. Contribute more to your health savings or flexible savings account. This reduces your taxable income and helps establish a healthcare **emergency fund**.

3. Contribute more to charity. Hey, it's the right thing to do, and you might be able to get a deduction on your taxes too, if you itemize (versus taking the standard deduction).

Tax diversity

While the above three strategies could help reduce your current taxes, there's another strategy I want you to consider as well: tax diversity.

Investing in a **Roth** IRA doesn't help your current tax situation because Roth contributions are not tax-deductible, whereby you are funding with after-tax monies. But a Roth account does grow tax-free and withdrawals are tax-free as well, meaning you paid the taxes before you made the contribution. Uncle Sam has no further claims on this money.

The decision as to whether or not you should contribute to a Roth account should probably be a discussion between you and your tax preparer. However, if your marginal tax rate is less than 25% (federal and state combined), then you might benefit from a Roth contribution; those withdrawals are tax-free in retirement, making them some of the most powerful dollars. Roth is so advantageous that the federal government limits how much you can contribute each year. Currently the limit, for an individual, is $7,500 annually.

Another way to add tax diversity is to do a Roth conversion. A Roth conversion is when you transfer money from a traditional (tax-deferred) **retirement account** to a Roth IRA or Roth **401(k)**. When you do this transfer, the amount of the Roth conversion is taxable. A Roth conversion might make sense if you have an especially low tax liability one year. For example, maybe you retire from full-time work one year and then work part-time the following year. You should consider a Roth conversion in the year you work part-time because your marginal tax rate is much lower than when you were working full-time. Boldin. com (formerly Newretirement.com) includes a helpful planning tool in evaluating when a Roth conversion could be most beneficial. Do some planning and consult your tax preparer as well.

If you have tax diversity in retirement, you can pull from accounts that are both taxable and nontaxable to minimize your effective tax rate. This is especially beneficial once you start taking Social Security, and once **required minimum distributions (RMDs)** kick in (around age 73). It's possible (but not likely) that your projected taxes in retirement could be higher than during your working career. It depends on many factors, including how many itemized deductions you had available during your working career. You might not have many itemized deductions in retirement.

How are federal income taxes calculated?

Tax brackets are a little wonky, so let's start with a simplified example (see Figure 14).

Gross income	100,000	
Pre-tax deductions (e.g., 401k)	15,000	
AGI, adjusted gross income	85,000	
Itemized/standard deduction	20,000	
Taxable income	65,000	
0-22,000	2,200	10%
22,001-89,450	5,160	12%
89,451-190,750	0	22%
Tax	7,360	
Child tax credit	500	
Income tax liability	6,860	
Witholding from paychecks	7,000	
Refund/(liability)	140	
Effective tax rate	6.9%	
Marginal tax rate	12%	

Figure 14: How Federal Income Taxes are Calculated

In this example, this household has a salary of $100,000 per year. This is their gross income before any taxes or withholdings (e.g., 401(k), medical premiums) are taken out. This is not their take-home pay.

Their total pre-tax deductions are $15,000. These withholdings come out of their paycheck (before income taxes are applied) before it gets deposited into their bank account. We'll assume they contributed $10,000 to their 401(k) and paid $5,000 in medical premiums.

The result of these pre-tax withholdings is an adjusted gross income (AGI) of $85,000. Let's further assume they have itemized deductions of $20,000; they had $10,000 in property taxes and $10,000 in charitable donations. If they're married and filing jointly, they might be better off taking a standard deduction, but I'll use $20,000 for simplicity.

This results in taxable income of $65,000.

The first $22,000 of their taxable income is taxed at a 10% rate, resulting in a tax liability for this bracket of $2,200.

Subtract $22,000 from their $65,000 taxable income to get $43,000. $43,000 gets taxed in the next bracket at 12%. The tax liability on this $43,000 is $5,160.

Their tax liability at this point is $7,360; however, they also qualify for a $500 child tax credit. Notice a tax credit reduces their tax liability dollar-for-dollar, as opposed to a tax deduction that only reduces their taxable income. A tax credit, therefore, is much more powerful than a tax deduction.

After applying the $500 tax credit, their final tax liability is $6,860.

Then we look at their paycheck and see that their employer withheld $7,000 of estimated income taxes. Since $7,000 is greater than $6,860, they are due a refund of $140.

Their marginal tax rate is 12%, meaning the next dollar they earn would be taxed at 12%.

Their effective (think average) income tax rate is 6.9%. The math behind this calculation is their total/final tax liability of $6,860 divided by their gross income of $100,000.

Some folks really enjoy getting a tax refund every year, but that means you loaned the government your money interest-free for the whole year . . . I'd rather you owe a little bit to the government, which means you received an interest-free loan. If you received a tax refund, work with your HR department to adjust your W-4 (withholding) form and get more in your paycheck each month.

Make sure you work with your CPA to identify all the tax credits you're entitled to. For example, there are child tax credits, energy-efficient tax credits, childcare credits, etc. Also, keep good records during the year, including:

- W-2s
- 1099s
- Brokerage statements
- Charity statements
- Home purchase closing documents
- Home improvement receipts, which might be useful for energy efficiency credits or to demonstrate an increase in basis, to avoid paying any tax on the sale of your home. The first $250,000 of gain is excluded from tax, but home improvement documentation reduces the amount of tax you pay should you sell it for $250,000 more than you originally paid.

HOMEWORK

Are there any steps you can take to minimize your taxes, now or in the future?

Chapter 17

INSURANCE: WHICH POLICIES DO YOU NEED?

Let's revisit rule #20 from chapter 1 and see which kinds of insurance you should get on your financial journey. Having the correct insurance is a key to **financial stability**, and its absence is a ticket to heartache.

1. Health insurance – one of the must-have policies you should get. Lack of healthcare coverage is a leading cause of bankruptcy. Most employers offer coverage to their full-time employees. By default, I'm going to gravitate toward a high-**deductible** policy because it's paired to an **HSA (health savings account** is triple tax-advantaged). Usually, high-deductible policies will have lower premiums. The reason a high-deductible plan saves you money is because you're self-insuring more. Make sure you contribute enough in your HSA to cover your deductible (could be over $4,000). If you don't have access to employer-provided health plans, then shop on the Affordable Care Act (ACA) Health Insurance

Marketplace and get some coverage for you and your family. Otherwise, one unexpected accident could lead to bankruptcy.

2. Life insurance – recommended for folks who have family members who depend on their salary for their living **expenses**. I especially recommend life insurance for the breadwinner when there are children involved. I strongly prefer term life insurance—it's much less expensive than whole/permanent life insurance, and when you're old enough, you can self-insure (lowers your expenses); your assets are sufficient to provide for your loved ones in the event you die earlier than expected.

> **Life insurance** is a contract with a financial company (e.g., MetLife) whereby the insured (you) pay monthly premiums to get life insurance coverage over a set period of time (e.g., twenty years). The policy value is paid to the beneficiary (e.g., spouse or children) in the event of the insured person's death. Life insurance is meant to replace someone's income/salary to those that are dependent on this salary (e.g., spouse and/or children). A common suggested amount of coverage is ten times the insured's salary.

> Universal/permanent/**whole life insurance** is a hybrid insurance product. Part term life insurance, part investment vehicle. Kinda the worst of both worlds in my opinion—expensive term life insurance and low **rate-of-return** on investment (maybe 2% or 3%); but it does have some tax advantages that might be beneficial to a very small portion of the population (i.e.,

very affluent). It has a cash value that can be borrowed against.

3. Auto insurance – a must have if you own a vehicle. It's the law in most states and makes sense regardless. At a bare minimum, you need to have liability coverage, which pays in the event you are found to be at fault in an auto accident. Comprehensive coverage is also recommended for new and gently used vehicles because if you're involved in an auto accident and have to replace the car, this is a significant financial event. If you have kept a car for greater than eight or ten years, once the value of the vehicle drops below $2,000, you might want to drop the comprehensive portion of the insurance and self-insure for that portion of a potential loss. Use some critical thinking and compare the cost of comprehensive coverage to the value of your vehicle. If the comprehensive coverage costs $800 and would only pay out $2,000 if you need it, then maybe you're better off self-insuring.

4. Disability insurance – provides a percentage of your income during a period when you're medically unable to work. Disability insurance comes in different varieties, but it mostly covers short-term disability claims at one rate, say 70% for up to twenty-six weeks, for example, then switches to long-term coverage after twenty-six weeks. Note there is sometimes an elimination/waiting period before coverage kicks in, so this does not replace your need for a healthy **emergency fund**.

Long-term disability might only replace 40% of your income while you are medically unable to work. Some coverage is for your specific occupation, while some only provide coverage if you are medically unable to do any occupation. Many employers offer disability coverage through your benefits options. If not, you can purchase from an insurance company. Check with your HR department to find out what's available. If you don't have any coverage options at work, then shop various insurance companies for the best rate.

5. Homeowners' or renters' insurance – might be required if you have a mortgage. While renters' insurance isn't required, I do recommend it in the event you need to replace your belongings due to an unforeseen situation (e.g., flood damage).

6. Identity theft insurance – recommend partly because it's inexpensive and partly because cybercrimes are all too commonplace nowadays. I haven't had to use my coverage but believe it would be very inconvenient and time-consuming should my identity be stolen.

7. Umbrella policy insurance – important protection if you are sued for more damages than your existing insurance covers. You pay premiums for secondary insurance coverage to protect you in the event of a large claim. This is additional insurance on top of your existing insurance—typically homeowners' and car insurance. This can prove beneficial if you are involved in a car accident (that you caused) and multiple drivers sue you for damages. Most car insurance policies will have a relatively low payout per individual accident. In other words, your existing car insurance most likely has a maximum amount it will cover. After this maximum coverage amount is reached, you are on the hook for

any additional liability. I recommend an umbrella policy once you reach your thirties or forties and have reached a modest **net worth**.

8. Long-term care insurance – not something I'm recommending, but I believe you should evaluate your situation (including family history) and consider whether this makes sense for you. I usually recommend folks self-insure for this possibility, mostly because the premiums can be prohibitively expensive and are likely to increase as you age. Self-insuring means having a fairly large nest egg. It could also involve selling your home. Skilled nursing is quite expensive—costs can exceed $100,000 per year, depending on the facility. The US congressional **budget** office estimates that 33% of individuals turning sixty-five will need long-term care for at least three months.

Insurance cost-reduction strategies

Increase your deductible. If not already there, explore the possibility of raising the deductible to $2,500. This should reduce the premiums you pay, allowing you to save money by self-insuring for the first $2,500. Be mindful, this strategy requires that you keep a healthy emergency fund to more than cover higher deductibles.

Shop for lower premiums every year. Many times your bank or **credit union** will shop for you. Sometimes it's beneficial to bundle several of your insurance policies. Price it both ways and get the best deal. Make sure to review your declaration of coverage page to make sure you're comparing apples-to-apples in a price comparison of different companies.

Know your home's worth. Keep in mind that over time, your home-owners' policy might not be adequate to replace your home should coverage be required in the event of a total loss. This shortfall is due to inflation, which increases the cost to replace your home over time. Check Zillow for an estimate of your home's worth, and then check with your insurance company to make sure you have adequate coverage.

HOMEWORK

1. Are there any insurance policies that you need but don't have?

2. Could you save money by raising your deductibles? How much could you save?

3. Have you recently shopped for insurance coverage? Are you able to pay less for the same coverage?

Chapter 18

RETIREMENT: ARE YOU READY?

W hen I was a teenager, I used to love to read *Choose Your Own Adventure* books. I was intrigued by the series of choices you got to make for the main character, like whether or not to go into an ominous-looking cave. Based on your choice, you would skip to another page in the book for yet another choice.

Retirement is sorta like that. Let's lay out four possible adventures you could choose, and imagine what each might look like:

1) Nightmare retirement
2) Burden to others retirement
3) Average retirement at 65
4) Financial freedom retirement

What if you have to retire early? It's a good idea to game plan how you would handle the situation if you were forced to retire five years earlier than planned. Forty percent of folks retire earlier than they anticipated due to circumstances beyond their control, per SmartAsset. This might be due to physical limitations you develop in your fifties or sixties. You might become disabled or have a chronic health condition that prevents you from working. Or maybe you need to stop working to care for a loved one.

Jimmy's 10-Point Retirement Checklist

1. <u>Are you retiring from something or to something?</u> I'm convinced we're designed to have a purpose; this applies to your retirement years just as much as it does in your twenties.

2. <u>Have you calculated your retirement expenses from the ground up as well as top-down?</u> Estimate your retirement expenses at 70% of your pre-retirement income (top-down approach), but switch to a detailed line-item **budget** (see chapter 2) when you are about five years away from your retirement date.

3. <u>How much of your expenses can you cover with your portfolio</u> (e.g., using a **4% safe withdrawal rate**) and **Social Security**? You'll want to choose a withdrawal strategy (see chapter 19) to ensure you have a sustainable retirement.

4. <u>What if you have to retire a few years early?</u> Plan for the possibility of retiring earlier, maybe up to 5 years, than anticipated.

5. <u>Have you run a Monte Carlo simulation to check your likelihood of success?</u> Stress-test your financial assumptions to see what happens in various scenarios. The future isn't set; a range of possible outcomes awaits.

6. <u>Do you have twelve-to-eighteen months of cash</u> to protect against **sequence of returns risk**?

7. <u>Do you have health insurance coverage?</u> You can apply for Medicare at age 65 but will need ACA or other coverage should you retire before then.

8. <u>Have you researched the best time to file for Social</u>

Security? Be sure to investigate Medicare coverage options as well.

9. Are you debt-free? I strongly recommend you are debt-free before you even consider retirement, especially early retirement, but personal finance is personal, so I'm sure some can be successful even if they are still paying off a small mortgage.

10. Do you have any major expenses coming up, like a new car, roof, or trip to Europe?

Hopefully something in the 10-item checklist above made you ponder your approach and priorities for retirement. Let me go over a few items in a little more detail.

You need to have a purpose in retirement.

I'm sure you can binge watch your favorite show on Netflix for a couple of weeks, but after that, you're going to be bored. Make a list of possible activities you might fill your time with. Maybe you still want some structure to your week. Perhaps take a non-stressful part-time job or a volunteer position.

What does your ideal day in retirement look like? What time do you get up? What activities are you doing during the day? Your vision might evolve somewhat as your retirement date draws near. Think about what you find tedious in your current job. Think about what you find rewarding and satisfying about your current job. What projects and activities could you undertake in retirement to minimize the tedium and maximize your satisfaction?

You might very much dislike the corporate grind or an overbearing boss, but you'll need a plan on how to fill your time or else your retirement might be a failure. Write down some possibilities and discuss them with your spouse or a close friend. Explore what you can do in the next, exciting chapter of your life.

I'm intrigued by some research done by Wes Moss. He discusses happy and unhappy retirees and postulates that happy retirees have around four "core" pursuits/activities, while unhappy retirees have less than two. These core pursuits/activities vary by retiree but mainly encompass their time and socialization. Moss defines core pursuits as "hobbies on steroids." He defines socialization as at least one organized social group that meets at least monthly. Examples of socialization might include: church, Bible study, pickleball, or reading (i.e. book club). The author stresses that your core pursuits need to be developed *before* you retire.

Calculate your retirement expenses

It's also important to get your finances right, or this too could lead to an epic fail. Your retirement expenses will almost certainly be lower than your pre-retirement expenses because you will no longer have: a mortgage, work-related expenses (e.g., work clothes, higher transportation costs), retirement contributions, life insurance, **disability insurance**, car payments, or student loan payments. I'd pencil in 70% (of your pre-retirement income) as an estimate of what your retirement expenses are likely to be (for planning purposes).

In the book *The Essential Retirement Guide* by Frederick Vettese, the author starts with a 70% assumption, based on the math behind defined **pension** plan assumptions. He goes on to suggest that your needed income in retirement varies based on a percentage of your final average pay. Middle- to upper-middle-income earners need 54% and 50% of their final pay, respectively, to cover retirement expenses. Upper class need only 45%. Lower income should target 70%–90%.

Vettese's findings are based on actual retiree spending, which drops pretty significantly as you age. For example, many retirees stop buying most durable goods (furniture, cars, etc.) in the final ten years. Because your spending drops as you age, especially in your seventies and eighties, the required nest egg to fund your retirement doesn't need to be as large (as the 4% rule suggests). I'd recommend 70% as a reasonable estimate, but you'll need to do a detailed ground-up budget once you're about five years away from retirement.

Let's do an example using Vettese's methodology: Average Joe made $100,000 as his final salary at age 65. We'll take 54% of his $100,000 to get $54,000 of income needed to fund his retirement **expenses**. Let's assume that Joe and his wife both file for Social Security and receive $30,000 in total annual benefits. $54,000 less $30,000 leaves a shortfall of $24,000. Using the 4% rule, let's estimate he needs a nest egg of ($24,000/.04) = $600,000.

One thing to keep in mind is that most retirees go through three phases: 1) go-go years (into your mid-seventies), slow-go years (say 75–80), and no-go years (let's say 80+). In each stage, your expenses are likely to step lower, except for the last few years when you will likely have higher medical costs. The empirical evidence from existing/ previous retirees strongly suggests you will not need 100% of your pre-retirement expenses throughout your retirement years.

Put together a retirement budget, including both your expenses and sources of income. Estimate how much Social Security income you will receive (from ssa.gov, see chapter 12). If you're reading this and you're under 50, I recommend you reduce the Social Security benefit estimate by 25% to be conservative. Social Security is likely to go through some changes in the next decade or two due to funding challenges, beginning around 2030. I'll cover withdrawal strategies in the next chapter, but use a 4% or 5% withdrawal rate for planning purposes (for now).

Put it to the test

Once you have set a preliminary budget, stress-test your assumptions using a Monte Carlo simulation. There are several online tools that can help you do this. I recommend Boldin.com, but Empower.com is another good option. A Monte Carlo simulation runs 1,000 different scenarios using historical data and gives you the likelihood of success. If it comes back with something less than a 70% success rate, then revisit your income and expense assumptions, or possibly your **savings** rate or your retirement date.

Don't retire without the cash

I strongly recommend you have twelve-to-eighteen months of cash (in a **high-yield savings account**) prior to giving your retirement notice. Having a healthy cash balance will allow you to sleep at night and avoid having to pull money from the **stock market** when stocks are declining (a "bear market"). If you retire when stocks are in a freefall, then you will have sequence of returns risk. Without a healthy cash cushion, you could be withdrawing at the worst possible time, and this could lead to running out of money in retirement (i.e., the nightmare scenario). You will probably want to get a little more conservative as well in retirement, maybe by increasing your bond allocation and decreasing your stock allocation. I don't think I'll get super conservative until I'm in my mid to late sixties, at which point I might be on a glide path to a 60/40 or 50/50 stock/bond portfolio (70 and beyond maybe).

Investigate insurance coverage options

I recommend you meet with a Medicare expert when you reach the age of maturity (age 65). There are many different Medicare options, and I'm not qualified to review them for you, but there are professionals that do just that.

Jet-setting in your plans?

You might not have a complete picture of your retirement financial **needs** if you neglect to consider upcoming, large, one-time expenses. Don't skip this step. If you identify them in retirement, you will need to game plan how you're going to pay for them that doesn't involve debt.

Debt is bad enough during your working years but can be devastating to recover from during retirement.

Final thoughts

Your version of retirement might involve a part-time job or not. Don't let someone else define your version of retirement.

My retirement mantra is plan, plan, plan, then plan some more. The old cliché is measure twice, cut once. Once you have left the workforce, it might not only be disappointing but extremely difficult to reenter after you have been retired for a couple of years.

I also encourage you not to keep moving the goal posts, unless it's a mathematical correction/update for a bad assumption. It's a big transition, but fear/momentum shouldn't intimidate you into working a year or two past your financial freedom date. Don't waste your go-go years with a few more years in the office. This will most likely lead to regret.

Once you've successfully navigated Jimmy's 10-point Retirement Checklist and you're sure you're ready, you'll need to choose a withdrawal strategy. But that's a topic for the next chapter.

HOMEWORK

1. Project your monthly expenses in retirement, using 70% of your current income as an estimate. Calculate how much of these monthly expenses will be covered by your Social Security benefit and your portfolio income.

2. Are you saving enough for your desired retirement? Choose from the four options at the beginning of this chapter.

3. If you are within five years of retirement, do a detailed estimate of your monthly expenses and run a Monte Carlo simulation. Sign-up for a software solution such as Boldin.com or Empower.com to complete your Monte Carlo simulation. What is your likelihood of success?

4. What's your plan if you should have to retire five years earlier than your desired retirement age?

5. Discuss your plans for your purpose and activities in retirement with your spouse or a close friend.

Chapter 19

RETIREMENT WITHDRAWAL STRATEGIES

You've completed the **retirement** checklist (chapter 18) and checked all the boxes. You're ready! You've been **saving** and **investing** for decades, but now comes the big question: How much can you safely withdraw from your nest egg without running out of money? Depleting your funds in retirement is one of the biggest fears retirees have. Getting the withdrawal rate right, well it's kind of a big deal.

In 1994, financial advisor William Bengen published a study that tried to answer that very question—how much can I safely withdraw? He concluded you could safely withdraw 4% of your portfolio and not run out of money. For example, if you had a $1,000,000 nest egg, then your initial withdrawal (year one) would be $40,000. In year two, you would adjust the $40,000 for inflation. If inflation was 3%, then the year two withdrawal would be $40,000 times 1.03, which equals $41,200. And so on. Four percent is only used in year one; after that it's static except for inflation adjustments.

The FIRE community savings goal is based on a **4% safe withdrawal rate (SWR)**. If you save 25 times your annual **expenses**, then you are set for the 4% SWR. $40,000 times 25 equals $1,000,000. The 4% SWR and the Rule of 25 are essentially the same thing.

Bengen found that a 4% SWR lasts for at least thirty years, fifty in most cases. Even those scenarios that failed to last fifty years lasted at least thirty-five, which appears more than adequate if you retire beginning at age 60 to 65. If you retire at age 65 and are retired for thirty-five years, then you are celebrating your one-hundredth birthday. According to the US Census Bureau, the average retirement is eighteen years.

Bengen used some assumptions in his study. He used a 50/50 portfolio of stocks and **bonds** (intermediate treasuries). He used market returns from 1926 through 1992. A 10.3% average return for stocks and an average 5.2% return for bonds. Bengen didn't factor in fees in his analysis. If you utilize a low-cost index fund, then these fees are relatively inconsequential, and the 4% SWR should hold up. However, if you're using an advisor who charges 1% (common **AUM** fee), then a 4% SWR might not last. If you use active mutual funds, which have higher fees than index funds, this too might cause the portfolio to fail. The 4% SWR assumes a rigid/static withdrawal rate, but there are alternatives to this static rate, which we will explore below.

My biggest complaint about the 4% SWR is that retiree spending usually steps down during retirement as retirees go through the three phases: go-go years, slow-go years, and no-go years. Because of this, the 4% SWR can result in a large portfolio at death. From my perspective, you could/should have spent more in the go-go years when you were still healthy enough to better enjoy the fruits of your labor.

Let's explore some alternatives to the 4% SWR.

1. Spending guardrails – setting upper and lower limits. You start with a 5% withdrawal, and then in year two, calculate how much the inflation-adjusted withdrawal is as a percentage of the portfolio. Six percent is the upper

limit with a 4% lower limit. These upper and lower guardrails add some flexibility based on actual market returns. This is essentially financial planner Michael Kitces's simplified version of #4 below.

2. <u>Spending safely in retirement strategy</u> – involves two components: 1) Delay claiming **Social Security** until age 70. If there is a spouse, they might choose to file early (62 is the earliest you can claim your Social Security benefit). 2) Calculate the portfolio withdrawal using the same formula as used for **required minimum distributions (RMDs)**. RMD is an IRS formula based on the 12/31 balance from the previous year, divided by a life expectancy factor based on your age.

   RMD – required minimum distribution. The amount of the annual RMD is based on the fair market value (FMV) of your **retirement account** at 12/31 of the previous year. This retirement account FMV balance is then divided by an IRS-determined life expectancy factor (a.k.a. RMD divisor) for your age. Let's do an example. Joe has a traditional IRA worth $1,000,000 at 12/31/23. Joe is aged 72. His life expectancy factor is 25.6 (per an IRS table that gets updated periodically). Therefore, take $1,000,000 divided by 25.6 to get $39,062 (3.9%) to calculate his minimum distribution. Note Joe doesn't have to spend this money, but he does need to take the distribution out of his account and pay the associated income taxes.

3. <u>5% withdrawal rate</u> – each year, you calculate 5% of the 12/31 balance from the previous year. This accounts for market activity whereby you take larger distributions when the market has a good year and smaller

distributions when the market has a bad year. This is somewhat problematic because it makes it more difficult to plan since your distributions will necessarily fluctuate from year to year.

4. Guyton-Klinger spending decision rules – calculates annual distributions based on four rules: 1) portfolio management, 2) withdrawal, 3) capital preservation, and 4) prosperity. The portfolio management rule is based on which investments a retiree takes their annual distributions from (there's a preferred order). The withdrawal rule says you can take an inflation adjustment each year except when the portfolio had a negative return, and the current year withdrawal is a higher percentage than the previous year. The capital preservation rule states that annual spending is cut by 10% if the current withdrawal rate exceeds 20% (growth) of the initial withdrawal rate (e.g., 5% to 6% is 20% growth). Finally, the prosperity rule allows you to increase annual spending by 10% if the current withdrawal rate falls below 20% of the initial withdrawal rate. Essentially, this allows an initial withdrawal rate as high as 5.6% with a 99% chance of success. See #1 above for a simplified version of this approach.

5. Annuities – one way to determine your income in retirement. Some will turn their entire portfolio over to an insurance company and get a paycheck-like income stream each month. For example, a 70-year-old man buying a single premium **annuity** can lock in a fixed 8.6% annual payout rate (per blueprintincome.com as of December 2024). If this 70-year-old man pays the insurance company $1,000,000 (lump sum payment

up-front), then he will receive a guaranteed $86,002 annually ($7,168 per month) for the rest of his life. Some select an immediate annuity at age 80 to avoid having to worry about running out of money.

The major downside to this approach is that once the money is turned over to an insurance company for an annuity, it's gone. This is a permanent decision. This money cannot be left as an inheritance or spent on a home purchase for that matter. You're essentially purchasing a lifetime **pension**. With an inflation adjustment rider, it is very similar to your Social Security benefit.

Due to this downside, my recommendation is to limit your annuity exposure to 5%–10% of your retirement portfolio. One school of thought is to combine Social Security and a small annuity to cover your basic living expenses, earmarking the remainder of your retirement portfolio to cover discretionary retirement expenses.

6. Three-bucket strategy – "now," "soon," and "later" buckets. The "now" bucket is two-years-worth of expenses (not already covered by a pension or Social Security) held in a money market or high-yield savings account; the "soon" bucket is money you will need in three-to-nine years, typically invested in bonds, treasuries, CDs, or other low-risk investments (maybe even ultra-safe dividend stocks); and the "later" bucket is money you won't need for nine plus years. This is the growth bucket, maybe an **S&P index** or total stock market index.

If you only need your portfolio to last fifteen years, the Financial Planning Association says you can have a 7% withdrawal rate (not inflation-adjusted) with a 100% chance of success (50/50 bond/stock allocation). An 8% withdrawal rate has a 99% success rate.

While the 4% rule and Rule of 25 might be the simplest when trying to determine your retirement savings rate during your working years, a more dynamic withdrawal rate might make more sense once you're retired.

I haven't determined which withdrawal strategy I will use, but I'm leaning toward #2 above, the "spend safely in retirement" method. My current plan is to have my wife take her Social Security at age 62, while deferring my benefit to age 70. I like the simplicity of this approach. Defer Social Security to age 70 and take RMDs for the rest of my retirement funding. RMDs are calculated each year, which takes into account current market conditions. I think this dynamic approach allows for better alignment with market conditions, which seems more prudent. I confess I'd be comfortable with a 5% initial withdrawal rate, maybe even 6%, assuming you have at least 50% of your portfolio invested in stocks.

Some struggle with the transition from saving money to spending money. You've probably spent the past three or four decades saving for retirement. Now that the day has finally arrived, it might be difficult to flip the switch and start spending down that nest egg. But the nest egg was designed for your benefit in retirement. Time to enjoy the fruits of your labor!

HOMEWORK

Which withdrawal strategy sounds the most appealing to you? Why?

Chapter 20

MISTAKES I'VE MADE AND OTHER BLUNDERS YOU SHOULD AVOID

Don't pay the stupid tax!

Mistakes. We all make 'em. But what are the top 10 financial blunders? I think I've made eight of these mistakes. Doh! I was being stupid in a no-stupid zone. The crazy thing is, you can recover from your financial mistakes. Turn over a new leaf. Turn those bad habits into good habits. How? One decision at a time and day-by-day. *The Money Guy Show* suggests you make the good decisions easier (e.g., automate), and the bad decisions (e.g., **credit card debt**) more difficult.

Wealth is built little by little (Proverbs 13:11). Get your spending under control. Get a part-time job and pay off that stupid tax. Learn from your mistakes; better yet, learn from others' mistakes and don't make the blunder in the first place. Ramsey Solutions estimates that personal finance is 80% discipline/behavior (you already know you should spend less than you make) and 20% knowledge. Sounds about right to me.

I can't help you with the discipline part—that's up to you! Choose each day to live for the future (stay on **budget**). Delay gratification. Save up for purchases. Take a tip from **millionaires** and sleep on a purchase before you pull the trigger, especially a major purchase. A 24-hour delay can make the difference between a good decision and a nightmare purchase that could haunt you for years. Talk to a close friend who is good with money. Don't talk to your broke cousin who can't hold down a job. Everyone should be tracking their **expenses** monthly and telling their money where to go and what to do.

Top 10 financial blunders (per the Principal Financial Group Annual Financial Well-Being Index 2016)
1) Not saving enough
2) Accumulating credit card debt
3) Spending outside my means
4) Taking on more debt
5) Investing too little in my retirement
6) Not budgeting properly
7) Draining my emergency fund
8) Failing to invest
9) Investing at the wrong time
10) Taking out a 401k loan

Let's take a closer look at these blunders and how you can avoid them.

Failing to invest/Not saving enough/investing too little in my retirement/investing at the wrong time

I recommend **saving** 20% of your salary for **retirement** (including any **company match**). Twenty percent assumes you start fairly early (in your twenties) and relies on the power of **compounding** and a diversified portfolio, invested mostly in stocks (index funds). If you have a **401(k)** with a company match, start contributing right away! Only one-third of those with access to a 401(k) actually contribute anything. What gives? Revisit chapter 10 if investing is one of your weaknesses.

Accumulating credit card debt/spending outside my means/ taking on more debt

Set a balanced budget. Setting a budget is simple—I didn't say it was easy—but it *is* simple. Spend less than you make. Start with the basics: food, housing, and transportation; then pay any debts you owe (e.g., student loans). I only recommend adding luxuries (don't confuse **wants** with **needs**) once you are debt-free (excluding your mortgage). If you really want that new couch, then save up and pay for it in full. Don't put it on a **credit card**. My point is to budget for your needs before you consider budgeting for your wants. I know this is challenging, but overcoming the stupid tax is a game changer; it will take hard work, discipline, and time.

Harness your passion, develop your perseverance; in short—get some GRIT (see an excellent video below). This 5-minute video demonstrates that stamina and perseverance pay off. It's a must watch video.

- https://shorturl.at/QBNdc

Track your expenses, manually or via an app. I'm old school and use an Excel spreadsheet with a different tab for each month, along with the EveryDollar budgeting app. If budgeting is a real struggle, or you end up going over in certain categories, then go retro and use an old-fashioned envelope system (a.k.a. **cash stuffing**)—yep, cold, hard cash! Set up an accountability partner—your spouse or a close friend (you can trust)—to help keep you on track.

Draining my emergency fund/failing to budget properly

Draining your **emergency fund** is not a problem if it's truly an emergency. Examples of emergencies include: car repair, house repair, unplanned medical expenses, etc. Examples of expenses that are *not* emergencies: a smartphone, a vacation, the latest Xbox, etc. If you do drain your emergency fund, make sure to put at least $1,000 back—as soon as you can! I recommend three-to-six months living expenses after you are debt-free (excluding your mortgage).

Taking out a 401(k) loan

This is technically your money but you end up getting taxed twice because you are repaying a 401(k) loan with after-tax money, and you will get taxed again when you withdraw in retirement. You could also end up with tax penalties if you change jobs before you pay it back. Plus, you are unplugging that money from being invested and short-changing the power of compounding. Unless they are on the verge of repossessing your house, don't do it!

My biggest financial weaknesses

I decided to reflect on those financial areas of my life that tend to trip me up the most. They say honesty is the best policy, but this might be taking it too far.

- <u>Spending on family.</u> I admit I sometimes go overboard trying to "provide" for my family. I want them to have the best, and I'm sure I have spent more than I should. I believe my biblical desire to be a good father and husband are good and all, but I'm also sure that splurging on top quality (expensive) items is not really displaying good judgment. I insisted we get a large wooden playset in the backyard—of course it had to be made from redwood and cedar. It was thousands of dollars—can you say overkill?

I extended this same misguided philosophy to our dining room suite, had to be genuine Amish oak. My wife asked for a small shed for the mower, and I insisted on a sixteen-by-twenty shed with a loft. You get the picture.

- <u>Technology.</u> I like to think I need the latest iPhone every year. I suffer from frugality fatigue if I have to go more than twelve months with the same smartphone (imagine the world's smallest violin playing me a lullaby). I'm convinced we should replace our desktop computer— even though it works fine—just because it isn't the latest model with a superfast processor.

- Cars. Trust me—it's a bad idea to go into debt to finance a depreciating asset. That new car smell will cost you thousands and reduce your **net worth**. Don't do it! Buy a car you can afford, preferably with cash and worth no more than 20% of your salary.

- Poor planning. That's a sufficiently vague description, so I will elaborate with some examples. It's a surprise when I need to replace the tires on my car. Who knew they would wear out? Did I plan ahead, anticipate this obvious expense and set aside money into a **sinking fund**? *No, I did not*! I'm not a rocket scientist, simply not that clairvoyant. Did I set money aside when we had to replace our HVAC? You guessed it. That same brilliant planning pretty much applies to all our house-related maintenance and repairs. I'm the poster child for having a fully funded (i.e., three–six months) emergency fund.

This poor planning led to periodically carrying a credit card balance (That wasn't supposed to happen!). A couple of examples include an unexpected vet surgery and a bathroom reno that went over budget.

HOMEWORK

1. Consider your own personal financial journey. Have you made any of these mistakes?

2. What have you learned?

3. How can you make the good decisions easy and the bad decisions more difficult?

SECTION III

INSPIRATION AND NEXT STEPS

Chapter 21

WHAT DOES THE BIBLE SAY ABOUT MONEY?

There are over 2,000 verses in the Bible about money and possessions. This includes topics such as **wealth**, possessions, greed, monetary mindset, satisfaction, investment, and more.

I selected a few verses from The World English Bible (WEB) to illustrate the great wisdom contained in the Bible. I added my commentary in parentheses when the language was a little difficult to understand.

1. Hebrews 13:5, Be free from the love of money, content (*satisfied*) with such things as you have, for he has said, "I will in no way leave you, neither will I in any way forsake you."

2. Philippians 4:11-13, Not that I speak because of lack, for I have learned in whatever state I am, to be content in it. I know how to be humbled, and I also know how to abound. In any and all circumstances I have learned the secret both to be filled and to be hungry, both to abound and to be in need. I can do all things through Christ who strengthens me.

3. Matthew 6:21, For where your treasure is, there your heart will be also.

4. Ecclesiastes 5:10, He who loves silver (*money*) shall not be satisfied with silver (*money*); nor he who loves abundance, with increase: this also is vanity (*meaningless*).

5. Proverbs 22:7, The rich rule over the poor. The borrower is servant to the lender.

6. Romans 13:8, Owe no one anything, except to love one another; for he who loves his neighbor has fulfilled the law.

7. Proverbs 13:11, Wealth gained dishonestly dwindles away, but he who gathers by hand (*little by little*) makes it grow.

8. Matthew 6:24, No one can serve two masters, for either he will hate the one and love the other, or else he will be devoted to one and despise the other. You can't serve both God and Mammon (*money*).

9. 1 Timothy 6:10, For the love of money is a root of all kinds of evil. Some have been led astray from the faith in their greed, and have pierced themselves through with many sorrows.

10. 1 Timothy 6:17-19, Charge those who are rich in this present age that they not be arrogant, nor have their hope set on the uncertainty of riches, but on the living God, who richly provides us with everything to enjoy; that they do good, that they be rich in good works, that they be ready to distribute, willing to share; laying up in store for themselves a good foundation against the time to come, that they may lay hold of eternal life.

11. Proverbs 10:4, He becomes poor who works with a lazy hand, but the hand of the diligent brings wealth.

12. Revelation 3:17, Because you say, 'I am rich, and have gotten riches, and have need of nothing;' and don't know that you are the wretched one, miserable, poor, blind, and naked.

13. 1 Timothy 5:8, But if anyone doesn't provide for his own, and especially his own household, he has denied the faith, and is worse than an unbeliever.

14. Luke 16:11, If therefore you have not been faithful in the unrighteous mammon (*worldly wealth/money*), who will commit to your trust the true riches?

15. Ecclesiastes 11:2, Give a portion to seven, yes, even to eight (*don't put all your eggs in one basket, diversify*); for you don't know what evil will be on the earth.

16. Proverbs 13:22, A good man leaves an inheritance to his children's children, but the wealth of the sinner is stored for the righteous.

17. Proverbs 21:20, There is precious treasure and oil in the dwelling of the wise; but a foolish man swallows it up (*spend less than you make*).

18. Proverbs 3:9-10, Honor Yahweh (*God*) with your substance (*money/wealth*), with the first fruits of all your increase: so your barns will be filled with plenty, and your vats will overflow with new wine.

19. Deuteronomy 16:17, Every man shall give as he is able, according to Yahweh (*God*) your God's blessing which he has given you.

20. Luke 12:15, He said to them, "Beware! Keep yourselves from covetousness (*greed*), for a man's life doesn't consist of the abundance of the things which he possesses."

21. Malachi 3:8-10, Will a man rob God? Yet you rob me! But you say, 'How have we robbed you?' In tithes and offerings. You are cursed with the curse; for you rob me, even this whole nation. Bring the whole tithe into the storehouse, that there may be food in my house, and test me now in this," says Yahweh (*God*) of Armies, "if I will not open you the windows of heaven, and pour you out a blessing, that there will not be room enough for.

22. Haggai 1:6-7, You have sown (*planted*) much, and bring in little. You eat, but you don't have enough. You drink, but you aren't filled with drink. You clothe yourselves, but no one is warm, and he who earns wages earns wages to put them into a bag with holes in it. "This is what Yahweh (*God*) of Armies says: "Consider your ways.

HOMEWORK

1. Which verses spoke to you the most? Why? In what way?
2. Which verses do you struggle with the most? Why?

Chapter 22

TOP 10 HABITS OF HAPPY PEOPLE

I don't want your financial journey to make you bitter because of unreasonable sacrifices; rather, I want your financial journey to be part of your path to satisfaction. I want your financial decisions to become part of your habits, part of your lifestyle. Life is an adventure—live with passion, live with a vision of what your **financial independence** will look like one day. Live with a dream—live with a purpose!

Happiness, for some, is an elusive pursuit of a mirage in the desert—always within sight but just out-of-reach. For others, it seems to come naturally. What makes them different? I came across an article in *Forbes* magazine that ranked the top 10 habits they had in common. Let's dive right in and see what makes people happy.

1. <u>They slow down to appreciate life's little pleasures.</u> Enjoy the sunset, watch the fireflies, get outside.

2. <u>They exercise.</u> You already knew this one, they regularly schedule it and follow through.

3. <u>They spend money on other people.</u> Giving will change your perspective on life.

4. <u>They surround themselves with the right people.</u> Avoid negative influences.

5. <u>They stay positive.</u> Stop complaining so much.

6. <u>They get enough sleep.</u> This really helps with mood, focus, energy, and self-control, and reduces stress.

7. <u>They have deep conversations.</u> Avoid gossip and judging others; instead, build a connection with someone.

8. <u>They help others.</u> It's a positive influence on your mood, but don't overcommit.

9. <u>They make an effort to be happy.</u> Attitude is a choice— work at it.

10. <u>They have a growth mindset.</u> You can improve with effort; challenges are really opportunities to learn something new.

This list is a great way to review your own happiness level. Maybe there are a couple of opportunities you should pursue. Once you've checked off the boxes above, however, I want you to try to go further up and further in. I want you to level up from happiness to contentment. Happiness can be fleeting but contentment is a mindset.

Paul, from the Bible, said:

[11] Not that I speak because of lack, for I have learned in whatever state I am, to be content in it. [12] I know how to be humbled, and I also know how to abound. In everything and in all things I have learned the secret both to be filled and to be hungry, both to abound and to be in need. [13] I can do all things through Christ, who strengthens me. (Philippians 4:11–13)

Do you ever get tired?

I know I do. How do you recharge your batteries? I like to say that I suffer from frugality fatigue (*don't feel sorry for me, seriously . . . no one else does*).

When you're tired, you're tempted to make bad decisions. I think the key to turning your financial life around is to be content with what you have. Don't focus on what you see from others on Instagram and Facebook. Focus on *your* life—be content and don't try to live someone else's life. The definition of content per the Oxford dictionary:

> In a state of peaceful happiness. Willing to accept a particular thing; satisfied.

"When you are just EXISTING, life happens to you … and you manage; when you are truly LIVING, you happen to life … and you lead." — Steve Maraboli

May I humbly suggest you start each day with prayer and a Bible verse (the Holy Bible app will send it right to your smartphone). Be thankful for all the blessings you have and the opportunity to live another day. Also, you may want to start your day with a list of priorities. What are the most important things you need to accomplish today? Write them down and cross them off as you accomplish them. Say no to distractions (Facebook anyone?). You are only given so many days—make each one count! Be faithful each day, show up and play hard! Practice excellence. Never lose sight of your purpose. Evaluate your daily habits. Don't settle for mediocrity.

How do you define wealth?

Interestingly, most Americans cite a stress-free life and having "peace of mind" as their personal definition of wealth (*Bloomberg* article, May 2018). On the surface, this appears to indicate that many have a healthy view of life and don't believe acquiring vast amounts of money is the key to happiness. But I'm not so sure that's what these results really mean. I believe many would readily admit that money, *or rather the lack of money*, can be the cause of a great deal of stress.

Your personal definition of "peace of mind" might also include financial freedom. Is your personal attainment of contentment contingent on acquiring vast amounts of money? According to the 2024 Modern

Wealth Survey from Charles Schwab, Americans believe you need $2.5 million to be "wealthy." I believe you should set financial goals and have the self-control necessary to delay gratification in order to achieve your goals; however, I don't think your contentment should be contingent on having amassed such and such in your bank account. I want you to be content now! Life is a journey, not a destination.

Clearly, many Americans believe you can buy happiness. I will readily admit that a significant lack of money can be a stress-inducing situation, and I won't try to convince you otherwise. But each person's definition of "wealthy" appears to vary considerably, with 18% defining it as being able to afford anything they desired, while 17% said it is having "loving relationships with family and friends." I would argue that the pursuit of money is not a meaningful pursuit in and of itself. Many rich people have committed suicide. "Mo money mo problems" (renowned American philosopher, the notorious B.I.G.). They didn't have a purpose. They were just chasing the glittery things of this world.

For what will it profit a man if he gains the whole world and forfeits his life? Or what will a man give in exchange for his life? (Matthew 16:26)

Don't be conformed to this world, but be transformed by the renewing of your mind, so that you may prove what is the good, well-pleasing, and perfect will of God. (Romans 12:2)

Americans long for lives that don't revolve around money.

What is wealth to you? (per the second annual Schwab Modern Wealth Index)

- Living stress-free / peace of mind 28%
- Being able to afford anything I want 18%
- Loving relationships with family and friends 17%
- Enjoying life's experiences 14%
- Having lots of money 11%

- Having good health 7%
- Being charitable 2%
- Other 3%

What makes for a rich daily life?

- Spending time with family 62%
- Taking time for myself 55%
- Owning a home 49%
- Meals out/meals delivered 41%
- Subscription services like Netflix and Spotify 33%
- Grooming/pampering 29%
- Having the latest tech products 27%
- Shopping at specialty grocery stores 22%
- Having a busy social life 21%
- Driving a luxury car 21%
- Gym membership/personal trainer 17%
- Using a home cleaning service 12%
- Using a car service, not public transport 10%
- Other 4%
- None of the above 6%

49% of respondents said that **saving** and **investing** is "the key to wealth," with another 40% citing "hard work," and 11% citing "luck."

Think about it. . .

These survey results were revealing about how the average American thinks about wealth and their everyday decisions, and how they affect our happiness and contentment.

HOMEWORK

1. Do you believe there is a difference between happiness and contentment?

2. Are you content? Why or why not?

3. How do you define wealth?

4. Did anything in this chapter make you question your current priorities?

Chapter 23

10 THINGS I LEARNED FROM MILLENNIALS

Alright, alright, I'll admit it, I'm a little obsessed with millennials, a.k.a. Gen Y. Their mindset, their approach, their priorities—it all makes me curious about what makes them so different compared to other generations. Millennials question the status quo—why do I have to work forty hours a week when I can get my work done in thirty?

Specifically, I'm interested in how they approach personal finance. I'm convinced they are truly, significantly different from previous generations. I've been accused of throwing shade at millennials and will readily admit that some of their tendencies seem a little wonky (downright irritating actually, #YOLO—FALSE! You live every day, you only die once #YODO). Many are walking contradictions (aren't we all?). Having said that, this chapter isn't about being hypercritical of twenty and thirty-somethings—we were all young and inexperienced once.

I'm going to list the top things I have learned—and admire—about the millennial approach to finances, because truth be told, I'm a millennial wannabe. I'm just too old to be an actual member of the cool kids' club . . . Before I get to the list, let me state the obvious—these traits don't apply to all millennials. I'm not here to stereotype everyone born from 1980 through 1995. That would be crazy; however, there are some traits that are common among this generation—traits that set them apart from other generations.

Top 10 things I've learned from the millennial approach to personal finance

1. It's better to spend money on experiences than stuff. One survey (Harris Poll) indicates that 78% of millennials would rather spend money on an experience than on a desirable good. For many, they simply don't fall for the siren call of extreme materialism (McMansion, luxury sports car, etc.). Buying possessions could drain your bank account. This got me to thinking, what are some of my most memorable experiences ?

My top 10 experiences (It was really difficult to list only 10— I guess I'm rather nostalgic . . .)

1. Spring training baseball with my dad and Uncle Dale – in Florida near Orlando. There's really nothing quite like spring training baseball—a timeless American tradition.

2. UNC basketball game with my parents and my wife Heather – when Tyler Hansbrough broke the scoring record (Go Heels!).

3. Banff (Canadian Rockies) – hiking with friends to a frozen lake; 83 degrees at the base, then you hit the snow line after a 45-minute hike—amazing!

4. Alaskan cruise with family – spectacular views, the train, the whales, the glaciers, the rainforest, the reindeer, the smoked salmon . . .

5. <u>Disney vacation with my family</u> – Mickey, Star Wars, Indiana Jones, a safari ride, Epcot, international food and wine festival—priceless memories!

6. <u>Boat tour of Lake George with close friends</u> – beautiful mountain views in upstate New York. I could easily go back every year!

7. <u>Smith & Myers concert with a buddy</u> – probably the best concert I've ever been to—small venue, great vocals, and some of my favorite alternative rock songs from Shinedown, including lots of covers: Phil Collins, The Eagles, Adele, U2—you get the picture.

8. <u>Snorkeling in Georgetown</u> (Grand Cayman) with Heather on our honeymoon – the blue water, the coral, the fish—all in crystal clear high definition!

9. <u>The River Walk</u> in San Antonio with a mariachi band with Heather – hard to describe, but it's very picturesque—I love south Texas; Austin (live bands), the brisket (The Salt Lick), and of course the Alamo—everything is bigger in Texas!

10. <u>Snowmobiling near Lake Placid</u> with family and friends – it's intoxicating going through the snow, whether it's slowly to navigate trees or over 40 miles-per-hour on longer stretches.

I think millennials have a great point. I wouldn't trade any of these memories for, say, a new Beamer—not a chance!

2. <u>You can save money in a sharing economy.</u> Rent out a room in your house (Airbnb) and possibly bank a few thousand each year to help pay part of your mortgage. Use Uber and maybe you don't have to buy a car at all—might be workable if you live in a big city. Imagine the savings of no car payment, insurance, gasoline, maintenance, etc. Social networking sites like Nextdoor.

com make it easy for people to connect with others locally and share power tools or gardening equipment.

3. <u>Technology is your friend.</u> Cut the cord. Automate your finances. Millennials are comfortable with technology and are more willing to pay bills online and automate their **savings**.

4. <u>Restaurants are expensive—eat at home.</u> Millennials are increasingly shunning restaurants (especially chain restaurants versus their prerecession levels), and why not? You can get great ideas from Pinterest and cook at home— after going to the farmers' market to get some local, ethical, fresh flavor. A restaurant meal can easily cost $15–$20 per person versus $4–6 per person if you cook at home.

5. <u>You can earn some mad money from a side hustle.</u> A recent study (Bentley University) indicates that 66% of millennials want to start their own business. Maybe you want to start your own blog/podcast, provide online tutoring services, teach English remotely, be a social media/SEO consultant, pet sit, drive for Uber—there are a lot of possibilities . . .

6. <u>It's important to focus on learning in your career.</u> Lifelong learning can lead to a more fulfilling and healthier life. Interconnected millennials embrace technology and prioritize happiness and learning—they believe there is a link between the two. Millennials are constantly microlearning with so much information at their fingertips. This information helps their career aspirations.

7. <u>Optimism is paramount.</u> Millennials are persistently more optimistic than other generations about their prospects and the future. 80% think they will be better off than their parents (*Forbes*).

8. <u>Talking about money is not taboo.</u> Millennials are going to talk about their salary and finances and are unimpeded if other generations are uncomfortable with these typically forbidden subjects (The Cashlorette's survey). They are significantly more likely than other generations to discuss their salary with friends, family, and even coworkers. They are revealing and transparent—maybe in an effort to make the workplace more equitable. Knowledge is power—know your worth. Millennials use social media to ask for financial advice from peers—personal finance is a team sport!

9. <u>Simplifying is key.</u> This generation is more actively **frugal**, reconsidering the role of material possessions, luxury, and sustainability—probably as a result of the Great Recession (2007–2009). This new approach affects their shopping and consumption habits. Whether by necessity or by choice, minimalism is now en vogue. Basics are in—complexity and clutter are out. Recycled and vintage are chic. You have to be a minimalist to live in a tiny home. I think millennials are redefining **needs** and **wants** in pursuit of what's really important, which includes functional products with a lower environmental impact.

10. <u>Avidly saving and avoiding credit cards.</u> This might be a reaction to the Great Recession as well. A 2018 Bank of America survey found that 1 in 6 millennials had $100,000 or more in savings. That's impressive! One study (Bankrate.com) showed that about two out of three millennials didn't have a **credit card**. Another study (Facebook IQ) said that 46% of *millennials define financial success as being debt-free.*

HOMEWORK

1. What millennial traits inspire you?
2. What are some of your most memorable experiences?

Chapter 24

TOP 5 WAYS TO BECOME POOR (REVERSE PSYCHOLOGY)

D o you want to enter the ranks of the working poor and live **paycheck to paycheck**? Have I got a plan for you! I've ranked the top 5 ways to ruin your finances—reminds me of a funny movie from the eighties, *Brewster's Millions*. Richard Pryor had to spend $30 million in 30 days and have nothing but the shirt on his back after his spending spree.

Jimmy's Top 5 Ways to Ruin Your Finances

#5 Don't have a monthly budget or emergency savings (at least $1,000) set aside for a rainy day (e.g., roof repair, car repair, etc.). I have read a lot of books and articles about **millionaire**s, and one of the common themes is to give each dollar an assignment—tell your money where it should be going, otherwise your money will own you!

#4 Don't seek treatment for a drug or alcohol addiction. I don't think this requires a great deal of elaboration—drug or alcohol abuse is a significant problem and definitely a recipe for ruining your life, including your finances. Seriously, if this applies to anyone, AA is a great resource, and you should go!

#3 <u>Stick with unreliable transportation.</u> My limited research validates my theory that lack of reliable transportation is a strong predictor of a lack of upward mobility. This is probably pretty self-evident. My point is a little counter to conventional wisdom. Most personal finance experts (including many I deeply respect) recommend you pay cash for a car—for many that is getting the cart in front of the horse (IMHO). I personally would bless a car loan (20/3/8 rule, see chapter 6) if it advances one's upward mobility and **wealth** creation (your J-O-B). I absolutely think being debt-free is the goal of a successful personal finance plan, but it could prove significantly more challenging without the ability to get to work reliably and safely.

#2 <u>Become a single parent.</u> Single parents face significantly more financial obstacles than married families. I am a proponent of having children within marriage—I think it's financially wise and it's a biblical principle as well.

And finally, the number 1 way to consistently turn your finances into a hot mess (our southern term for a really bad situation, usually of your own doing) is, wait for it . . .

#1 <u>Spend more than you make.</u> Hey, it worked for Greece, Detroit, and Puerto Rico, and the US government has been consistently trying this winning strategy for years (over $35 trillion in debt and counting). The goal is to live beyond your means, max out your **credit cards**, and pile up as much debt as you possibly can: car loans, mortgages, student loans . . . you get the picture.

Honorable mention: An item that didn't quite make the top 5, but is sure to help with your poverty goal all-the-same:

<u>Don't graduate from high school</u> (college, fuhgeddaboudit). Lack of education is another great way to get, and stay, in the poor house your entire life.

HOMEWORK

Are you at risk for any of these mindsets?

Chapter 25

HOW TO PREPARE FOR A JOB LOSS

I'll be honest—I don't think I have all the answers on this one, but I'm going to give it the old college try and see if we can discover some steps you can take to be prepared (kinda-sorta-maybe) for the proverbial "pink slip."

Being prepared to lose your job isn't your typical financial problem. There are some financial steps you should take if this becomes your situation—more on that later—but I want to address the more philosophical aspect of this issue. To many, the prospect of being laid off is more than just a passing concern; it's an ever-present fear. It's a *recession* when your neighbor loses his or her job; it's a *depression* when you lose yours. This isn't really a math problem—you need to mentally prepare yourself for the real possibility, at some point in your career, that some business-case analysis will result in your position being eliminated (accountants call them *efficiencies*).

I have first-hand knowledge of this particular phenomenon. I was laid off in 2001 and will readily admit that being laid off can be quite disconcerting. For some, this can even lead to bouts of depression, as many see their job as an extension of themselves. Being laid off can be a form of rejection that some struggle to quickly recover from. I don't think it's particularly healthy to throw your very own pity party. I say mourn (briefly) and move on. I want to solve this problem with faith, friends, and preparation.

1. <u>Faith</u> – You all know by now that my faith is very important to me, and my self-worth is not wrapped up in my occupation. My job is not *who I am*—it's *what I do* to help support my family. I'm a Christian and believe my value comes directly from the Creator of the universe— He sent His Son to die for my sins (John 3:16)—to give me a hope and a future (Jeremiah 29:11). I could go on but don't imagine you tuned in for a sermon. For this reason, I remain cautiously optimistic.

   If I lose my job, I will find another—this too shall pass. Wisdom, guided by experience, has taught me this is so.

2. <u>Friends</u> – I recommend you confide in someone about your thoughts—warts and all; someone who will unconditionally love you and listen to your concerns, fears, and dreams. I believe God created us to be social creatures and don't think it's healthy to go through life alone.

3. <u>Preparation</u> – I believe there are many financial steps you can, *and should,* take in preparation of finding yourself unemployed:

   • <u>Build an emergency fund.</u> Most financial experts recommend you set aside three-to-six months' living **expenses.** This is sound advice as this cushion is designed to handle the proverbial "rainy day" that will certainly occur should you find yourself without a steady paycheck. If your company announces a merger (politically correct way of describing an acquisition), then I recommend making sure you have at least six months of living expenses set aside.

- Reduce your expenses. I think this is important for a couple of reasons. First, you might need to reduce your expenses to fully fund your **emergency fund**. Second, your next job might involve a lower salary and "right-sizing" your **budget** is a lot easier when you do it by choice, rather than by necessity. See chapter 4 for brainstorming ideas to cut back on your lifestyle.

- Update your LinkedIn profile and your resume. Regardless of a pending job loss, I strongly recommend you maintain a good network of business contacts (others in your industry, leaders, recruiters). You can learn from others (stay sharp!) and this network will come in handy should you need a reference or an idea of a good company to work for (following a layoff).

- Talk to a recruiter. In many industries, this a valuable way to learn about job opportunities. For example, Robert Half is a well-known financial job placement firm. They can also help assess what you can/should expect in a salary based on your skills, location, industry, etc.

- Read the book *StrengthsFinder 2.0.* – This leads you to an online assessment tool that helps identify your personal strengths and preferences to help narrow your job search to occupations you are best suited for. This could be a great opportunity to explore a different field or occupation; don't immediately take the next job that comes along. See chapter 8 for additional career tips.

These 5 steps are a good place to get started. I urge you to also consider how valuable an employee you are currently and consider ways to *become even more valuable*. Take the time, trust yourself, value yourself enough to ask your supervisor and maybe even a coworker.

It's difficult to find talented employees, so take the necessary steps to make yourself the best version of you possible.

Final thoughts

Be prepared to face the possibility of being laid off. If you're prepared, this forced change might even be a jumping off point to another exciting chapter in your life. Today's disappointment could be tomorrow's opportunity. Faith, friends, and a little financial preparation can lead to a brighter tomorrow.

HOMEWORK

1. Are you at risk of a job loss?
2. If so, have you taken any preparations?

Chapter 26

INSPIRATIONAL QUOTES

Quotes to motivate you along your **financial independence** journey. Some will inspire you, some will make you ponder, and some might even make you laugh.

- *Money can't buy happiness, but it can make you awfully comfortable while you're being miserable.*
  — Clare Boothe Luce

- *People who say money can't buy happiness obviously don't know where to shop.* — Gertrude Stein

- *Wealth, after all, is a relative thing since he that has little and wants less is richer than he that has much and wants more.*
  — Charles Caleb Colton

- *You can't go back and change the beginning, but you can start where you are and change the ending.*
  — C. S. Lewis

- *Take time to recharge your batteries. It's hard to see where you are going when your lights are dim.*
  — Robert H. Connelly

- *Successful people are always looking for opportunities to help others. Unsuccessful people are always asking, "What's in it for me?"*
  — Brian Tracy

- *Time is precious, waste it wisely.* — Ahsi Ayir

- *We make a living by what we get. We make a life by what we give.* — Winston Churchill

- *Everyone thinks of changing the world, but no one thinks of changing himself.* — Leo Tolstoy

- *Price is what you pay, value is what you get.*
  — Warren Buffet

- *Insanity, doing the same thing over and over again and expecting a different result.* — Albert Einstein

- *I admire your creative tax deductions and plan on writing you regularly when you go to jail for them.* — Unknown

- *One of the reasons people aren't rich is because almost everyone has more excuses than money.* — Robert Kiyosaki

- *Normal is broke, be weird.* — Dave Ramsey

- *Don't be afraid of being different. Be afraid of being the same as everyone else.* — Unknown

- *If you want to go somewhere, it is best to find someone who has already been there.* — Robert Kiyosaki

- *Difference between school and life? School teaches you lessons and then gives you a test. Life gives you a test and you learn the lessons.* — Tom Bodett

- *The only difference between a rich person and a poor person is how they use their time.* — Robert Kiyosaki

- *The rich invest their money and spend what is left; the poor spend their money and invest what is left.*

  — Jim Rohn

- *When you are young, work to learn, not to earn.*

  — Robert Kiyosaki

- *If you do what you've always done, you'll get what you've always gotten.* — Tony Robbins

- *Trying to be happy by accumulating possessions is just like trying to satisfy hunger by taping sandwiches all over your body.* — George Carlin

- *Too many people spend money they earned . . . to buy things they don't want . . . to impress people that they don't like.*

  — Will Rogers

- *Opportunity is missed by most people because it is dressed in overalls and looks like work.*

  — Thomas Edison

- *Money is a terrible master but an excellent servant.*

  — P. T. Barnum

- *You must gain control over your money or the lack of it will forever control you.* — Dave Ramsey

- *Investing should be like watching paint dry or watching grass grow. If you want excitement take $800 and go to Las Vegas.*

  — Paul Samuelson

- *If you don't value your time, neither will others. Stop giving away your time and talents. Value what you know and start charging for it.* — Kim Garst

- *Don't tell me what you value, show me your budget, and I'll tell you what you value.* — Joe Biden

- *If you live for having it all, what you have is never enough.* — Vicki Robin

- *Before you speak, listen. Before you write, think. Before you spend, earn. Before you invest, investigate. Before you criticize, wait. Before you pray, forgive. Before you quit, try. Before you retire, save. Before you die, give.* — William A. Ward

- *The **stock market** is designed to transfer money from the active to the patient.* — Warren Buffet

- *I'm only rich because I know when I'm wrong . . . I basically have survived by recognizing my mistakes.* — George Soros

- *If we command our wealth, we shall be rich and free. If our wealth commands us, we are poor indeed.* — Edmund Burke

- *The best thing money can buy is financial freedom.* — Rob Berger

HOMEWORK

1. Which quotes are the most inspiring? Why?
2. Do you disagree with any quotes? Why?

Chapter 27

PODCASTS AND PERSONAL FINANCE BOOKS I RECOMMEND

I'd like to share some of my favorite finance books and podcasts. While I am not endorsing all the concepts they espouse, they offer many helpful tips and are worthy of your valuable time. Many were sources of inspiration for numerous concepts in this book.

Personal finance books

The personal finance book/person that inspired my journey (saw him in person once): *Debt Free Living*, Larry Burkett

1. *Millionaire Next Door*, Thomas J. Stanley, probably my favorite

2. *The Next Millionaire Next Door*, Thomas J. Stanley

3. *Stop Acting Rich*, Thomas J. Stanley

4. *The Total Money Makeover*, Dave Ramsey, great approach to paying off debt

5. *Baby Steps Millionaires*, Dave Ramsey

6. *The Legacy Journey*, Dave Ramsey, Biblical perspective on finances

7. *Retire Inspired*, Chris Hogan, good motivational book to get you inspired to save for tomorrow

8. *Everyday Millionaires*, Chris Hogan

9. *Rich Dad Poor Dad*, Robert Kiyosaki questions conventional personal finance wisdom

10. *The Wealthy Barber*, David Chilton, interesting foundational personal finance book done via storytelling

11. *Love Your Life Not Theirs*, Rachel Cruze. Rachel emphasizes that comparison is the thief of joy

12. *The Essential Retirement Guide*, Frederick Vettese , actuary that studies retiree spending habits

13. *The Intelligent Investor*, Benjamin Graham, value investing 101

14. *You CAN RETIRE on Social Security*, Josh Scandlen, excellent review of Social Security benefits

15. *Your Money or Your Life*, Vicki Robin, foundational book on the FIRE movement

16. *Relax and Retire*, Josh Scandlen, good study of how inflation is calculated and what it means to your finances

17. *The Psychology of Money*, Morgan Housel, excellent psychological study of why consumers behave the way they do

18. *The Simple Path to Wealth*, J. L. Collins, His explanation of, and compelling argument for, index investing is excellent. FIRE proponent who promotes a pragmatic approach using a simple path to wealth, including why you don't need an investment manager.

Financial influencers and YouTubers I think are worthy of your time

1. *The Money Guy Show*, podcast and YouTube, excellent foundational personal finance channel, despite the fact that they're **AUM** investment managers

2. *Erin Talks Money*, YouTube channel, excellent foundational personal finance channel

3. retireearly500k, personal finance YouTube channel following a recent retiree who retired at 59 with $500K

4. Tae Kim, foundational personal finance YouTube channel

5. Two Sides of FI, conversation about FIRE movement from two guys, one who is close to FIRE and one who FIRED recently

6. Rob Berger, foundational personal finance channel, including worthwhile discussion on withdrawal strategies and how to use Boldin (formerly Newretirement.com).

7. *BiggerPockets Money*, good personal finance YouTube channel, especially their expertise on real estate investing, in particular Dave Meyer.

HOMEWORK

Are there any books or YouTube channels or podcasts you plan to check out? Which ones? Why?

Chapter 28

HOT TAKES

What is a hot take?

Per the Polly website:

"A hot take is a statement that's provocative enough that people can't help but weigh in with their thoughts. It's usually a controversial opinion that has no factually right or wrong answer, which means you can debate endlessly on who is 'right.'"

Jimmy's Financial Hot Takes:

1. Financial advisors/planners. Most anyone can call themselves a financial advisor; many are actually salespeople, sometimes only selling one product (e.g., **whole life insurance**). Many don't have your best interests in mind. Buyer beware! Only 11% of financial advisors offer comprehensive advice. They aren't looking at the big picture. By the time you know enough to select a good advisor, you will already know enough to manage your own finances. Don't complicate your life by paying expensive **management fees** and commissions to financial advisors that probably care more about

themselves (and their compensation). Even if you get lucky and find a good advisor, their fees are a big time drag on your portfolio performance. Keep it simple and invest in low-cost index funds instead. "Well intentioned but bad advice is endemic in this field. Advisors that put their clients' interests ahead of their own are 'rarer than baptized rattlesnakes.'"(J. L. Collins) **Assets under management (AUM)** is a common arrangement where your financial planner gets paid 1% (or more) of your **assets** as an annual fee. Many have a minimum amount of AUM before they will accept you as a client. Many won't accept you unless you have at least $500,000 or $1,000,000 of liquid assets that you turn over to them to manage on your behalf. If you have $1,000,000 of AUM, then you're paying $10,000 in fees each year, regardless of how well they manage your portfolio. According to J. L. Collins, an AUM fee of 2% decreases your portfolio return by 30% over 20 years. Craziness I say!

2. Buying silver or gold. Gold and silver don't produce anything (they just sit there looking pretty), so if you buy them, you're hoping you can sell them for more than you originally paid (per ounce). I'd say this is **gambling**, not **investing**. They are a store of value and are seen as a hedge against inflation. If you feel strongly about buying gold or silver, I'd favor silver because of its industrial applications. If you decide to buy, please limit to 5%–10% of your portfolio.

3. Buying Crypto. Crypto is basically digital gold (see #2 above), so I could support 5%–10% of your portfolio; however, buying crypto is still gambling.

4. **Credit cards**/rewards. Many credit cards offer rewards and rebates if you spend a certain amount annually. If you shop around, you might get 2% or 3% cash back or free hotel or flights. If you're spending the money on things you would have spent money on anyway, then the rewards could be a good deal. However, if you're spending more just to get the rewards, or worse yet, carrying a balance from month to month, then you're doing it wrong. Don't spend money just to get the credit card rewards.

5. Inflation. It's definitely a thing; government statistics might even underestimate its impact, depending on which measure you pay attention to. For many, their wages have not kept up with this higher cost of living. However, there are things you can do to help mitigate these higher costs. Reduce going out to eat. Go to lower cost restaurants. Order water with your meal rather than soda or alcohol. Share meals with a family member (American portions are too large anyhow). Order an appetizer as your meal. Select from the senior menu, if they allow it. Reduce your grocery bill: buy generic brands, use coupons, comparison shop, plan your meals for the whole week (before you go), and reduce expensive snack item purchases. These are just some ideas to help you offset inflation. Don't let high inflation derail your **saving** and investing goals.

6. **Annuities**. I'm not a big fan of annuities because they're fairly complex and are frequently layered with high fees and/or commissions. An immediate annuity might make sense for some, especially to supplement **Social Security**, to make sure you have your **basic living expenses**

covered in **retirement**. I'd limit annuities to no more than 20% of your portfolio.

7. Amazon Prime. As of this writing, the annual membership fee for Amazon Prime is $139. This cost might be worth it if you're getting good value. But be careful—Prime membership can be a gateway to spending more than you would otherwise, due to "free shipping." Amazon doesn't always have the best prices. Don't be lazy, shop around. Many times you can find the same item for less money elsewhere even when factoring in shipping costs.

8. **House hacking.** This is a viable option to keep your housing costs down, but there are trade-offs that should be considered before you go down this road. If you have a roommate or rent out half of a duplex (that you own), realize the risks, sacrifices, and work involved in maintaining this arrangement.

9. Car sharing. Similar to #8, this might make sense for some, especially those in bigger cities, where public transportation is well established. Realize there are risks and trade-offs related to renting your car to others (e.g., Turo).

10. Extended warranties. Generally, I am not a fan of extended warranties. I would rather you self-insure and avoid most of them. Warranties are expensive and might involve loopholes where the company isn't liable for certain claims. Buyer beware!

11. Costco and other membership clubs. See also #7 above. It could be beneficial to join Costco, or one of the other membership clubs. If you have spare room in a garage

or basement, maybe buying nonperishable items in bulk makes sense (if the price is right). Don't buy excess perishable items and let them go to waste.

12. Remote/hybrid work. I think remote/hybrid work is here to stay because the decreased office space required reduces company costs. Employees should be cautious though; working remote exclusively could be a career-limiting move. If some of your coworkers are hybrid or in the office full-time, they might be more likely to get promoted versus someone who works fully remote.

13. **Credit unions**. I'm a pretty big fan of credit unions because they usually have more attractive interest rates for loans and savings accounts. Big banks have a checkered past related to ethical violations, unattractive rates, and poor customer service. I recommend searching for local credit unions. There might be one available you could join.

14. High-yield money market funds. I'm a fan of shopping around and finding the best rate on a **high-yield savings account** or high-yield money market fund (you can find 5% as of mid-2024) rather than blindly accepting a low interest rate on your existing savings account (which might be less than 1%). Realize there is a little more risk associated with high-yield money market funds versus FDIC-insured high-yield savings accounts.

15. The latte effect. This is a term that refers to spending too much for your daily caffeine fix. Maybe you get a large caramel macchiato most days on the way to the office. The argument is, that $5 daily latte would be better invested in your **retirement account**. I won't argue with the math behind this analysis; however, if you get great satisfaction

THE MIDDLE-CLASS MILLIONAIRE

from your daily visit to Starbucks, I say go for it. Be mindful of the **opportunity cost**, but you're more likely to get better bang for your buck making wise decisions on your housing, transportation, and food budgets than eliminating your daily Starbucks run.

16. Separate accounts (married couples). I'll go from preachin' to meddlin' and strongly suggest you have a joint checking account. **Budget** for all income coming in each month from both spouses. You're on the same team! You can have line items (in your budget) for some individual mad money, but I believe you should be transparent with your spouse.

17. Childcare. It can be extremely expensive nowadays. Be smart about how much you spend in this area. I know the safety and well-being of your child is paramount, but don't blindly spend based on emotion. Maybe one parent or a close relative can stay home with your children rather than reflexively relying on dual incomes and public daycare. Use some critical thinking and be strategic.

18. 529 plans/saving for college. I recommend saving some for your children's college education. However, the cliché is true: you can get a loan for college but you can't get a loan for retirement. Don't automatically spend all your hard-earned money to pay for Jonny's out-of-state tuition to a private university at the cost of saving and investing for your own retirement. Try to budget to help Jonny go to an in-state college and continue to invest for your retirement. Maybe Jonny should get a part-time job in college and possibly a small student loan (no more than his first year starting salary). See also chapter 9.

19. <u>Support for adult children.</u> This is a sticky wicket. You might feel compelled to help provide financial support for your adult children, but be smart about it. Set some limits and communicate timeframe expectations. Help educate your children about smart financial decisions (send them this book). I don't think you should provide support indefinitely unless there is a permanent medical limitation or a special needs child.

20. <u>Inheritance planning.</u> I think it's commendable if you are planning to leave an inheritance for your children, but realize that generational **wealth** usually only lasts a generation or two, as your children and grandchildren will probably blow it.

21. <u>Elder care attorneys.</u> It's smart to consult with an elder care attorney if you are facing financial issues with elderly parents. Each state's laws are a little different; there are situations when Grandma leaves Sallie a house as an inheritance, but the state steps in and forecloses on Sallie because Grandma went on Medicaid (e.g., to pay for assisted living).

22. <u>Day-trading.</u> This is gambling, not investing.

23. <u>Life trusts.</u> Research these with the help of an attorney. They can be useful in certain situations, like those involving a special needs child, for example.

24. <u>Private schools/home schooling.</u> See also answer to #17 above. You might be dissatisfied with the public school options in your area and resort to private or home school. This might be the right decision for your family, but consider the financial implications too, as some options might be beyond your resources.

25. Retiring abroad. This might be enticing to some given the lower cost of living in many parts of the world (e.g., Thailand or Vietnam). Carefully consider the trade-offs before moving away from friends and family. The benefits, according to the brochure, might not fully account for the risks and sacrifices.

26. Timeshares. Buyer beware! I can't think of a good reason to purchase this expensive arrangement where fees can escalate over time with no easy way to exit this contract. I recommend you steer clear.

27. DIY home/auto repair. This is a viable way to keep your housing and transportation costs down; however, I recommend you stick to your circle of competence and not tackle projects beyond your ability. Maybe you believe you can fix a leaky faucet only to find out your repair efforts resulted in flooding your basement. Don't just jump on it yourself or reflexively call the $150 per hour plumber for everything. Do your research; there's probably an instructional video on YouTube on how to do some basic repairs.

28. Coupons. Coupon-clipping is a viable way to reduce costs, especially grocery bills, but realize this isn't passive and requires a fair amount of effort and planning on your part.

29. Biking to work. This might be enticing to some. The idea is to find housing close to your job and then bike to work (maybe you won't even need a car). In many cases, I think this involves too much risk. I don't trust the driving ability of the general public. Plus, your coworkers might not appreciate a sweaty office mate. I'd rather you find

other ways to reduce your transportation budget that involve less risk. See also chapter 6.

30. <u>Extreme early retirement in thirties/forties.</u> Retiring in your thirties/forties might be viable for some, but there are tremendous trade-offs and your goals might change if/when you start a family. Maybe you were able to live an extremely **frugal** lifestyle before you got married and had kids, but then your extreme frugality turned downright miserly. I recommend you enjoy each season of your life. See also chapter 14 on the FIRE movement.

HOMEWORK

Which hot takes do you agree with, disagree with? Why?

Chapter 29

WAYS TO MEASURE FINANCIAL SUCCESS

I believe the following six checkpoints, found in a 2017 *Forbes* article, are useful references to *challenge the status quo.*

In finances, you aren't competing against your neighbor or your coworker; *you are competing against yourself!* Are you making progress toward your goal of **financial independence**? *Or are you getting in your own way?* Let's walk through the following six steps and see if there are any areas you need to work on.

1. <u>Your net worth.</u> The article suggests you check this once a year. Write this down and see how you are doing from year to year. Is your **net worth** going up or down? Remember that net worth is everything you own (e.g., house, **401k**, etc.), minus everything you owe (e.g., mortgage, student loans, **credit cards**, etc.). *The Millionaire Next Door* formula for your net worth is your income times your age, divided by 10. If you're age 50 with a $100,000 salary, your net worth "should" be $500,000.

2. <u>Your credit score.</u> An excellent credit score will result in a lower interest rate, and that can make a big difference. A good credit score is an

indication of paying your bills on time and conscientiously paying off your debt. I would rather you not have any debt at all, but if you already have debt, don't neglect your credit score and end up paying more in interest. The article suggests a very good score is 740 (and higher). A 6.8% 30-year mortgage on a $430,000 house would have over $579,180 in interest over thirty years! That same 30-year mortgage would include about $684,360 in interest at 7.8%. Going from 6.8% to 7.8% on the mortgage will cost you an extra $105,180 (for the same house)! A better credit score can also reduce your insurance cost (in certain states).

3. <u>The number of months your emergency fund will carry you.</u> Most **financial planners** suggest three-to-six months' worth of living expenses be saved in a savings account (preferably a **high-yield savings account [HYSA]**). What would happen if you lost your job or had another financial emergency, like a costly medical issue or necessary home repairs (e.g., a leaky roof)? Would this involve lots of **credit card debt**?

4. <u>Your retirement saving percentage.</u> **Millionaire**s on average invest at least 20% of their income, according to *The Millionaire Next Door*. (see also chapter 10).

5. <u>Your debt-to-income ratio.</u> To calculate your debt-to-income ratio, take the total of your monthly debt payments (e.g., car payments, student loans, etc.) and divide it by your gross monthly income. According to Bankrate.com, lenders look for a target debt-to-income ratio of 36% or less. What's yours?

6. <u>Your giving percentage.</u> Personally, I believe a true measure of personal financial security is the ability to give. I don't just say that as a Christian (Christ was a giver, John 3:16, just sayin'). Giving will change your perspective on life—I promise. Remember, "it's not about you" (Pastor Rick Warren). Research even indicates that giving to oth-

ers makes us happier than spending money on ourselves. Regardless of your faith, I would encourage you to consider how you can give to worthy causes and give back to your community.

Money in and of itself isn't a goal. Money is a tool. Give careful consideration to how you use it.

As you improve and grow your **wealth**, it will be rewarding to look back and see how far you've come.

One way to measure how much you've improved and how far you've come is to think about the different levels of wealth. See below example of what these levels involve.

5 levels of wealth (per *The Money Guy Show* YouTube/podcast)
1. Stability
2. Strategy
3. Security
4. Financial Freedom
5. Abundance

1. Stability. In the first level of wealth, you have moved past just getting by. In the stability level, you are no longer **living paycheck to paycheck**. You're starting to pay down any credit card debt as you are practicing **deferred gratification** and living on less than you make. You've set up a starter **emergency fund** and could handle a $1,000 emergency without incurring credit card debt.

2. Strategy. In the second level of wealth, you're intentionally **saving** and **investing** (chapter 10) a portion (working up to 20%) of your income. You have a fully funded emergency fund with three-to-six months set aside in a HYSA. You've automated your 401(k) contributions each month. You are actively seeking to increase your personal finance knowledge. You have a **budget** and are in control of your money.

3. Security. In the third level of wealth, you've been saving and investing 20%–25% for a few years and compound growth has been allowed the time to work its magic. You've developed some good investing habits. You've been increasing your net worth for years now. You're probably paying cash for your next car, which is a little nicer than the basic Toyota Corolla you were driving previously. You've probably accumulated over $100,000 in your nest egg since you've been saving and investing for several years now.

4. Financial Freedom. In the fourth level of wealth, you've achieved financial independence and work is now optional. The income from your retirement nest egg is higher than the salary at your job. You might have changed from a full-time corporate gig to a part-time job that more closely aligns with your passion. Maybe you're Financially Independent, Recreationally Employed. You have accumulated twelve-to-eighteen months of cash reserves. You're probably totally debt-free, including your mortgage. See chapter 18 for a more comprehensive retirement checklist.

5. Abundance. In the fifth and pinnacle level of wealth, money is merely a tool. You have enough. You have achieved contentment, satisfaction, and fulfillment. You're comfortable with who you are and what your purpose is. You prioritize relationships and making the world a better place.

Milestones by age

Let's take a look at another way to measure your financial progress—Fidelity's milestones by age, which enables you to see if you're on track as you approach retirement age.

The ultimate goal is to save 10 times your pre-retirement income by age 67.

1X income at 30

3X income at 40

6X income at 50

8X income at 60

10X income at 67

I think these are useful milestones, but they are top-down estimates and are, therefore, somewhat inaccurate. The milestones for ages 30, 40, and 50 seem pretty accurate. Those for ages 60 and 67 seem too high, especially as your income grows late in your career. By the time you're 50 or 55, you can more easily estimate your retirement **expenses**: detailed by line item (i.e., bottom up approach). I prefer you shift to 25 times your retirement expenses (not covered by **Social Security**) once you're about five years away from retirement.

HOMEWORK

1. How are you doing using the six ways of measuring your progress?
2. How are you doing relative to the Fidelity age milestones?
3. What level of wealth are you currently in?

Chapter 30

IS IT TIME FOR A CHANGE?

An expert, by one definition, is someone who has already made all the mistakes. By that definition, I suppose I am an expert in personal finance because I've made most, if not all, of the mistakes.

I want you to get mad (at me)!

Seriously, I really do. I want you to take a long, hard look at your financial decisions. I hope at least one of my chapters has made you *question my sanity*. I hope it also made you question (at least ponder) your financial strategy. I'm hoping at least one of my chapters made you feel a little uncomfortable (*maybe even guilty?*). Are you uncomfortable enough to change? If you have read my book and I didn't challenge at least one of your financial habits, then I would call that a huge waste of time (similar to Betty White's description of the time sink that is Facebook).

I know some of my recommendations sound a little radical, but remember:

"If you do what you've always done, you'll get what you've always gotten." —Tony Robbins

Don't be an optimistic procrastinator. Waiting a little bit longer to get on the right financial path won't make your decisions any easier.

I realize you probably think some of my recommendations are extremely challenging—I agree! Personal finance is simple, but definitely not easy. Sometimes I struggle to make smart financial decisions. I am frequently preaching to yours truly, in search of determination and willpower to do the right thing; to do what it takes to get ahead (the right way).

Financial independence is difficult

Our society usually has more excuses than valid plans to improve our finances. I'm striving to help us overcome these excuses—excuses that only serve to encourage a life of mediocrity. Let's review a few of these excuses/myths:

1. Budgeting is hard and takes way too much time. It actually used to be a lot more difficult and time-consuming; but it turns out, there's an app for that. I personally use the EveryDollar app. Start with the basics: food, transportation, and housing—probably two-thirds of your **budget** right there (see chapters 2 and 3 to review getting started on your **budget**).

2. I simply can't afford a mortgage. I will admit, it's not easy. I still recommend you limit your monthly mortgage payment to, at most, 25% of your income. This way your mortgage allows you to live your life now (sorta) *and* hopefully not bring your mortgage with you into **retirement** (that's one friend you don't need tagging along). See also chapter 5.

3. It's simply not reasonable to ask me to buy a car that's only 20% of my income. You might be right again! Used car prices have increased in the last few years and this

indeed might be an area that you end up going over budget; however, your budget is a zero-sum game—if you go over in one area, you have to be under in another to compensate. Chapter 6 goes into more depth about cars, but to oversimplify, I strongly encourage you avoid going into debt for a depreciating asset. If you already have a car payment on an expensive car, consider selling it and buying a less expensive car (especially if you have **credit card debt**), or alternatively, keep the car—if you can pay off the note in two-to-three years.

4. It's too difficult to reduce my spending on food. I too struggle in this particular arena. I encourage you to limit your food budget to 10% of your total **expenses**. You can find tips about food budgeting at usda.gov. If you don't have the time (*or the inclination*) to do that much research, then start by limiting your dining out—eating at home is much less expensive than eating at a restaurant. You already knew that—moving on. Eat healthy though—you only get one body. It's not that life is too short, it's that you're dead for so long . . .

5. I don't need to set goals. Goal-setting is an essential part of the secret sauce you will need to be successful in the short, medium, and long term. Start small and set a goal to create (*and keep!*) a monthly budget (*every month!*). Set a medium-term goal to pay off your credit card debt and those evil student loans. Set a long-term goal to be **debt-free** (freeeeeeeeeedom!). Tell someone you are setting these goals and give them permission to hold you accountable. If you are married, this is a great opportunity to sit down and communicate (you can binge Netflix later); set these goals together—remember, you and your spouse are a team!

HOMEWORK

Which concepts in this book do you disagree or struggle with? Why?

CONCLUSION

I don't think writing is about creativity as much as it's about having the patience to discover those ideas worth passing on. I've shared useful knowledge and practical strategies that have helped me along my personal financial journey. I hope they do the same for you. I hope they help you achieve *your* financial success.

So you might be thinking, what's next? Keep reading. Keep learning. But don't go it alone. Consider reaching out to a financial coach.

Why do you need a financial coach? Because patterns are difficult to discern when it involves our own behavior. We see patterns in others much easier. Ideally, this pattern recognition will help you examine the gap between who you are and who you hope to be. That's the role I'm hoping to provide as your financial coach.

<u>Financial coach</u> – provides personal finance advice, guidance, education, and feedback to do-it-yourself investors, and is compensated by clients on an hourly or fixed fee. A financial coach has the heart of a teacher. A financial coach does *not* actively manage investments or determine financial decisions for you. They mentor and provide consulting style advice only.

Please visit my website at www.jimmysmoneytips.com if you're interested in taking our relationship to the next level.

You've got this!

JIMMY'S GLOSSARY OF PERSONAL FINANCE WORDS AND PHRASES

4% rule – concept that you can use a 4% safe withdrawal rate during retirement and not run out of money. The 4% rule is based on a 30-year retirement and assumes 50% **bonds**, 50% stocks. Each year, you can withdraw 4% of your portfolio to fund your living **expenses** (adjusted for inflation). This is a conservative approach to the amount you can safely withdraw. The 4% rule is the inverse of saving 25 times your expenses. I believe the 4% rule is overly conservative because it assumes your retirement expenses go up each year in retirement. Research indicates there are three phases of retirement: 1) the go-go years (maybe until age 75), the slow-go years (maybe until age 80), and the no-go years (age 80 and beyond). Research indicates retirement spending resembles a smile, highest right after retirement, drifting lower, until higher medical expenses occur the last couple years.

401(k)/403(b) – IRS designation for tax-deferred (i.e., pay the tax later, usually in retirement) accounts. Note you will pay the tax eventually but contributions to a 401(k)/403(b) tax-deferred retirement account reduce your taxable income in the year your contributions are made. 401(k)/403(b) accounts are available through an employer-sponsored savings plan.

annuity – an insurance product whereby you pay the insurance company, typically a lump sum, in return for a stream of payments in the future. There are many types of annuities, including immediate, deferred, and variable. An immediate **annuity** is the simplest. For example, a 70-year-old man buying a single premium annuity can lock in a fixed 8.6% annual payout rate (per blueprintincome.com as of December 2024). If this 70-year-old man pays the insurance company $1,000,000 (lump sum payment up-front), then he will receive a guaranteed $86,002 annually ($7,168 per month) for the rest of his life. Some select an immediate annuity at age 80 to avoid having to worry about running out of money.

asset (financial) – something you own that has financial value; typically can be sold (i.e., converted to cash) somewhat easily. Examples include houses, cars, bank accounts, etc. Some **assets** go down in value (depreciate) over time (e.g., cars), while others go up in value (appreciate) over time (e.g., houses, stocks, bonds).

assets under management (AUM) – where a **financial planner** (or their firm) charges a fee to actively manage your portfolio of assets and investments. A typical AUM fee is 1% of assets under management. For example, if you sign over a $1 million portfolio to a financial planner to manage for you, then you will pay a $10,000 annual fee—regardless of the **rate-of-return** that the portfolio earned that year.

average income/middle class – median household income in the United States is approximately $80,000 (2023 census); a common definition of middle class is 30% below (~ $56,000) and 100% above (~ $160,000) the median (per the Pew Research Center). There are many different definitions of middle class in the United States, but I use the $56,000–$160,000 range for simplicity/convenience.

(basic) living expenses – necessary costs related to needs, including food, shelter, and any **fixed commitments** (e.g., car payment, student loan payment); does not include discretionary costs. These are the monthly expenses you would have if you lost your job; basic living expenses are the minimum level of cost needed to fund your lifestyle.

BLS Consumer Expenditure Survey – a US Bureau of Labor Statistics report on average consumer spending. This data is collected annually and published each September. Reports can be found at bls.gov/cex. There are many reports/categories, including age, household size, income range, etc.

bond – a loan to a company or government that must be repaid with interest (a.k.a. the coupon). Most commonly, the interest is paid monthly or quarterly, with the principal being returned at the end of the term (e.g., ten years). Interest is usually quoted as a percentage. Recently, the 10-year US treasury bond was paying 5% interest. Therefore, if you loaned the US government $100 (for ten years), then you will receive $5 of interest income annually for ten years, then you will receive your original $100 back at the end of the term. The 5% interest rate doesn't change over the life of the bond. Certificates of deposit (form of a savings account at the bank) operate the same way. Note that during the term of the bond, you cannot access the principal. You only receive the principal back at the end of the bond term.

bridge account – investment vehicle funded with after-tax dollars, typically housed at a brokerage financial institution. The purpose of a bridge account is to fund living expenses from early retirement until age 59.5, which is the earliest age that you can access retirement accounts.

budget – a monthly plan, designated before the month starts, for how to spend your income. Start with your take-home pay (that goes into your bank account), then subtract necessary (e.g., food, shelter, transportation) as well as discretionary expenses (e.g., entertainment, restaurants). The plan allocates how to spend every dollar that comes into your possession. This includes recurring (e.g., mortgage/rent) as well as nonrecurring (e.g., couch). A budget is for both **needs** and **wants**; however, it should prioritize needs over wants.

cash flow – describes the cash coming in (e.g., paychecks) and out (expenses) during a period of time. Cash flow timing matters because you can't withdraw money not yet in your bank account. It's important to plan for and around the timing of paychecks and monthly expenses to avoid being overdrawn on your account, meaning you have spent more money than was available in your account. Being overdrawn results in significant fees from both your bank and the vendor you attempted (and failed) to pay.

cash stuffing (a.k.a. the envelope system) – budgeting technique where you divide your paycheck into envelopes using cash. For example, you put $200 into an envelope for groceries. You go to the grocery store with the $200, and if you go over $200, then you put some items back to get under the $200 limit. Digital payments can desensitize you to the amount you're actually spending.

cheap – being excessively stingy/miserly; ungenerous; hoarding your wealth; usually applies to how you spend and give of your money. Also applies to how you spend on yourself. The cheapest pair of jeans probably isn't the most **frugal** solution. A good pair of reasonably priced jeans might last longer than the cheapest pair, which might wear out much sooner. Being cheap is often short-sighted.

credit card – an open line of unsecured credit, where a financial institution allows the user (you) to spend a certain amount on anything you choose. In return, the credit card issuer/lender (e.g., VISA/bank) demands repayment. If paid back in thirty days, then there are no additional fees—just the original amount borrowed. If not paid back in thirty days, then the user is required to pay the original amount plus interest (20% APR is common). If you only pay the minimum amount each month, it will typically take seventeen years to repay the loan, including a significant amount of interest. That $1,000 couch will actually cost you around $3,000 if you make the minimum payments over the next seventeen years.

credit card debt – any remaining credit card balance that is not paid off within thirty days of purchase; the amount of the credit card balance that rolls over to the next month and is subject to an interest calculation.

credit union – similar to a bank; however, a credit union has members rather than shareholders. Credit unions typically have lower expenses than a traditional bank.

company match – employer contribution to your retirement account, usually to a **401(k)** or 403(b) account. If you (the employee) contributes 6%, then (and only then) the company (your employer) might offer a 100% match up to 6% (the cap or maximum match); then you will receive a dollar-for-dollar match. This is an incentive to encourage you to contribute to your retirement account. The free money in this example doubles the contribution (amount invested) from 6% to 12% of your salary. Different companies offer different matching percentages. Check with your benefits department for your specific **company match**.

compounding – term describing how money grows. The original amount invested increases over time as earnings/growth add to the original amount; then there is growth on top of growth. Over time, it's astounding how much it will grow. For example, $1 invested when you are 20 will become $77 by the time you're 65, using 10% compounding growth. $2 invested at age 30 will only become $59 by age 65. Even though twice as much was invested, it had less time to compound (grow). In the first example, $76 of the final $77 came from compounding/growth; that's over 99% of the final amount that came from growth.

debt snowball – paying off the smallest debt, then moving on to the next one, and so on. This method of debt repayment is based on the size of the debt rather than paying off the highest interest rate first.

deductible – refers to the portion of a claim that you have to cover (first) before the insurance company will pay you on your claim. This is the self-insured portion of the claim. This is common in health, homeowners', and car insurance, etc. You have to pay a portion (the deductible) before the insurance coverage kicks in. A higher deductible results in lower premium payments.

deferred gratification – delaying or putting off, until later, discretionary (i.e., not currently necessary) expenses. For example, you really want to take a Caribbean cruise. If you defer your trip until you have saved up the money and can pay for it, then you have deferred your gratification. The opposite of deferred gratification is putting the cruise on a **credit card** and hoping you can pay for it later. Deferred gratification requires tremendous willpower. The opposite is present bias, where you spend money you don't have on current wants/pleasures.

disability insurance – a contract with an insurance company where you pay premiums for disability coverage so that you receive a percentage of your income (e.g., 67%) during a period when you're medically unable to work.

diversification – spreading your investments among several options. The idea is that by **investing** in several companies or types of investments (e.g., stocks, bonds, real estate), you can reduce risk and volatility, and achieve more steady returns over time. The concept is that if you're truly diversified, your investment returns depend on different factors. For example, if there is a recession and all your investments go down together, then you weren't diversified. Typically, stocks and bonds rely on different factors for their returns. Historically, bonds have exceeded the return of stocks during a recession; however, over longer periods of time, stocks perform better than bonds. Other forms of diversification include gold, annuities, etc.

dollar-cost averaging – the concept of investing into stocks each month. This allows you to buy when the market is up and when the market is down—always be buying; this consistency avoids trying to time the market, which is typically a vain pursuit (unless your first name is Warren and your last name is Buffet).

emergency fund – money saved/set aside, typically in a **high-yield savings account** (very available, very safe). The purpose of this money is for important, unexpected needs (e.g., car, roof, or furnace repair). A starter emergency fund is $1,000. Graduate to cover your highest insurance deductible, then to a fully funded three-to-six months of living expenses.

expense – any cash outflow for cost of living (benefits occur in the current period/month); does not include saving and investing cash outflows, which benefits the future.

financial advisor – provides financial services or guidance to clients. Most any person can call themselves a financial advisor; many are actually salespeople and don't really have your best interests in mind. A good financial advisor is a fiduciary and puts your interests ahead of their own. Some advisors have passed exams designating them as certified financial planners (CFP).

financial coach – provides personal finance advice, guidance, education, and feedback to DIY investors, and is compensated by clients at an hourly or fixed fee. A financial coach has the heart of a teacher. A financial coach does *not* actively manage investments or determine financial decisions for you. They mentor and provide consulting style advice only.

financial freedom/independence – being totally debt-free and having saved 25 times your annual expenses. For example, $40,000 annual expenses times 25 equals $1 million. When your investment income (e.g., the 4% **SWR**) is greater than your monthly expenses, then you have reached financial independence (FI).

financial planner – directs/manages their clients' personal finances.

financial stability – the first stage on the path to financial freedom, where you have enough income to pay your bills on time (i.e., no late fees and no **credit card debt**). Your income is greater than your monthly expenses (**margin**), creating the opportunity to save and invest for the future. Financial stability includes at least a starter **emergency fund** to cover unexpected expenses. Financial stability includes some level of resilience to small shocks/disruptions. For example, a minor, unexpected car repair (e.g., $200 flat tire) doesn't result in credit card debt.

FIRE movement – Financial Independence, Retire Early – lifestyle movement first introduced by the book *Your Money or Your Life* (by Vicki Robin and Joe Dominguez). It usually involves a combination of an aggressive saving/investing rate (50% or more is common) and **frugal** living expenses. Most FIRE believers use the **4% rule** (a.k.a. Rule of 25) whereby you withdraw 4% of your **retirement portfolio** (in perpetuity) to fund your **basic living expenses**. Once FIRE is achieved, paid work is optional. There are many flavors of the FIRE movement, including: Lean (more **frugal**), Fat (less **frugal**), and Barista (involves recreational part-time employment during retirement).

fixed commitments – monthly expenses that are known and measurable based on previous decisions. Examples include mortgage, rent, car, and student loan payments.

forced scarcity – self-imposed spending limitation where you live on less than you make; Intentional saving/investing occurs automatically (paycheck withholding or recurring bank transfer) prior to utilizing income for monthly expenses.

frugal – being intentionally cost efficient in your lifestyle; simple living, not flashy, extravagant or luxurious; buying high-quality items but keeping them for a long time.

gambling – speculative investment, usually involving something you have purchased that you hope will be more valuable to an unidentified future buyer. It typically involves purchasing some store of value (e.g., crypto or artwork). Since it's speculative, it involves a high degree of risk (rather than knowledge) and is more akin to a game of chance. See also **investing** definition.

health savings account (HSA) – only available with a high-**deductible** medical plan. The IRS sets the maximum amount you can contribute annually because it's triple tax-advantaged. $8,300 was the maximum a family could contribute in 2024. Many use their HSA as a sinking fund to pay for their current medical expenses; however, you could invest HSA funds much like a mutual fund and use for future medical (e.g., during retirement) expenses.

high-yield savings account (HYSA) – bank account used to house your cash savings that has a better-than-average interest rate. In 2024, there were several online banks paying 5% interest on their savings accounts. A typical bank savings account pays around .5% interest (or less). Bank savings accounts are insured by the government (up to $250,000 per account), meaning you won't lose any money, even if the bank fails (i.e., goes bankrupt). Most people don't move their money from a traditional savings account to a HYSA because they're lazy and not paying attention to better options.

house hacking – a method of reducing your monthly housing expense by renting out a spare room or portion of your home.

investing/investments – utilizing savings to purchase stocks, bonds, or other **assets** that are likely to go up in value over time, at a rate greater than inflation. Investments typically involve risk (value might go down). Some investments have a stated **rate-of-return** (e.g., 5% bond) while others do not. For example, a stock's return (i.e., earnings yield) is its annual earnings divided by the price you paid for the share of stock. The **stock market**'s rate-of-return has been about 10% historically over longer periods of time (e.g., 15–20 years or more).

living paycheck to paycheck – state of being that results in only having enough income to pay basic living expenses, whereby you don't have enough income to save and invest for emergencies, discretionary expenses (e.g., vacation) or retirement. If you were to be laid off, then bills would pile up since there are insufficient savings to pay existing bills. Many would describe this lifestyle as barely getting by, highly dependent on employment income.

long-term care insurance – a contract where an insurance company pays for the insured's skilled nursing need, should one arise. The insured must pay premiums to keep coverage in place. Premiums frequently increase as you age. Sometimes these premium increases can become prohibitively expensive.

management fees – an expense you must pay a company to manage/ direct an account. For example, you might pay Fidelity a 1% fee as a mutual fund manager. Most retirement account fees are paid via lower investment returns; this method is somewhat hidden from the owner of the account unless they read the investment disclosures (i.e., the fine print).

margin – the positive **cash flow** that results from spending less than you make. Start with your income (e.g., paychecks), then subtract all your monthly expenses. If you have margin (money "left over"), then you have an opportunity to save and invest for the future. You can create margin by increasing your income (playing offense) and/or reducing your expenses (playing defense).

median – a more representative measure of average. Median is the middle. 50% of the population is below the median and 50% is above. Average is less accurate because it's skewed by billionaires. For example, the average household income in the US (2023) is about $100,000 but the median is $75,000.

millionaire – a person (or household) that has a net worth (assets less liabilities) of at least $1 million. It does not require a certain level of income.

money market fund/account – a repository for highly safe and highly available cash, which is typically invested in ultra short-term treasury notes (US bonds).

Mr. Market – a euphemism describing the stock market. Over the past 100 years, the stock market has had about a 10% rate-of-return; however, that's an average and there are periods of time when the stock market does better and others when it does worse.

needs – necessary expenses, including: basic shelter/housing, food/groceries, basic transportation, healthcare, basic clothing.

net worth – everything you own, less everything you owe; the positive financial value resulting from adding up all you own (e.g., house, car, 401(k)) and subtracting everything you owe (e.g., debts, student loans, credit card balance,). It's possible to have a negative net worth. For example, if you own very little but have $100,000 in student loans, then your net worth is negative. *The Millionaire Next Door* formula determines a benchmark (what your net worth should be if you're good at converting income into wealth). This formula is your age times your income, divided by 10. For example, if you're age 50 and have a $100,000 salary, your net worth should be 50 X $100,000 X .10 = $500,000.

opportunity cost – the loss of potential gain from another possible choice. The cost or thing you are giving up by spending money on one alternative versus another. If you spend $40,184 on a new car, you are forgoing the benefit of investing that same $40,184 in the stock market (i.e., another possible choice). That same $40,184 could grow to $1.8M if allowed thirty-five years of **compounding** (10% interest). The opportunity cost is the thing you can no longer achieve because you chose to spend this money on something else.

payday lender – a short-term lender of last resort. Payday lenders loan you money until you receive your next paycheck, at which point you pay them back the amount you borrowed, plus interest and fees. Payday lenders charge excessively high rates of interest and fees, so using them is strongly discouraged. Using a payday loan can be a vicious cycle, where you continue to need loan after loan just to get by.

pension – a retirement vehicle typically funded exclusively by the company / employer for the benefit of the employee upon reaching contractual age and tenure requirements. Pensions are defined benefit plans rather than defined contribution plans (e.g., 401(k)). Some traditional pensions pay out a certain percentage of the employee's final pay. A traditional pension plan is most similar to Social Security, where you receive monthly payments for the rest of your life. Many nontraditional (more common nowadays) pension plans are cash balance pensions and are more similar to a 401(k) plan, where there is a balance that goes up each month with both compensation and interest credits (e.g., based on the 30-year treasury rate). A cash balance pension is portable and is yours to keep once you have reached the required work/vesting (e.g., five years) requirements. Typically, a traditional pension is not portable and only applies if you work for the same company for most of your career. Pensions are relatively rare nowadays but can still be found in many state and federal occupations as well as some utilities.

PMI – private mortgage insurance. Most commercial banks (not **credit unions**) require PMI if your house down payment is less than 20%. PMI is mortgage insurance paid by the homeowner that benefits the bank in the event you default on your mortgage. PMI protects the lender, not the buyer. In theory, PMI results in lower interest rates to the buyer. Usually you can stop paying PMI once you have achieved 20% equity in your home. A typical annual PMI amount is between 0.5% and 1% of the loan amount.

rate-of-return – earnings expressed as a percentage of the original amount invested. For example, you invest $100, and a year later the bank pays you $110; $10 of interest in addition to returning the original $100. $10 of return (interest income in this case) divided by the original investment of $100 results in a 10% rate-of-return.

rebalancing – the periodic adjustment required to get back to a desired portfolio allocation. Say Joe wants to maintain a 60/40 portfolio of stocks and bonds. But after a significant stock market decline, his portfolio is 50/50. Joe would sell bonds and buy stocks to get back to his desired 60/40 portfolio allocation. Rebalancing in retirement is one way to take advantage and buy stocks when they are "on sale."

retirement – period of time after you stop working full-time, typically utilizing funds set aside during your working years to pay for retirement expenses. Retirement might entail working part-time/recreationally. Traditional retirement age is considered 65.

retirement account – any vehicle set aside for retirement expenses. This might be a tax-deferred account such as a 401(k) or a traditional IRA (contributions are tax-deductible), or an after-tax account such as a Roth IRA (contributions are after tax but earnings aren't taxed upon withdrawal) or a brokerage account. Or it could be a self-directed IRA— to hold gold, crypto, real estate, etc. Most retirement accounts charge fees, which are typically paid via a lower rate-of-return, making fees somewhat hidden.

retirement portfolio – all the assets or investments dedicated for funding retirement. This typically involves stocks, bonds, and money market funds, but might also include real estate, gold, annuities, etc. Investments (e.g., stocks, bonds, etc.) earn a rate-of-return while assets (e.g., gold, crypto) do not necessarily earn a rate-of-return.

RMD – required minimum distribution; IRS mandated distribution/ withdrawal from a tax-deferred account (e.g., 401(k)). RMDs don't apply to Roth IRAs. Basically, the IRS allowed your 401(k) and traditional IRA accounts to get funded and grow tax-deferred. But at age 72 (starting age in 2023), you must start taking RMDs, which are then subject to income taxes. The IRS hits you with a Draconian 50% penalty if you don't take your RMDs. The amount of the annual RMD is based on the fair market value (FMV) of your retirement account at 12/31 of the previous year. This retirement account FMV balance is then divided by an IRS-determined life expectancy factor (a.k.a. RMD divisor) for your age. Let's do an example. Liz has a traditional IRA worth $1,000,000 at 12/31/23. Liz is aged 72. Her life expectancy factor is 25.6 (per an IRS table that gets updated periodically). So take $1,000,000 divided by 25.6 to get $39,062 (i.e., 3.9%) in a minimum distribution. Note Liz doesn't have to spend this money, but she does need to take the distribution out of her account and pay the associated income taxes. Upon withdrawal, her financial institution will give Liz a 1099-R to include with her tax return.

Roth IRA/401(k) – a tax-preferred vehicle that is funded with monies that have already been taxed; these after-tax contributions are typically invested in stocks and bonds and are to be utilized to pay for living expenses in retirement. They typically can't be withdrawn until 59.5 years of age—early withdrawal usually involves fees and penalties. If you think your tax rate is higher in your working years versus your retirement years, it is preferable to utilize a traditional IRA/401(k) to get the tax deduction now; if you estimate that your tax rate will be higher in retirement, then pay the tax now and withdraw from a Roth account in retirement (tax will have already been paid at the time of contribution). Many believe in tax **diversification**—investing in both traditional and Roth accounts—to have options to withdraw from different accounts to minimize taxes during retirement. The government limits Roth contributions, and its availability can be curtailed for high-income earners.

S&P index fund – an investment vehicle composed of the 500 largest companies in the United States. There are many S&P index funds that have low fees; an index mutual fund is passively invested. There is not a manager actively deciding which companies to invest in; you are passively investing in the S&P index, meaning you won't beat or trail the "market" returns; you will achieve the market return itself while paying very low fees. Index fees are usually less than .2%, while some active funds charge up to 2.5%. Over time, large fees cause a significant reduction in the amount of the investment you get to keep. Historically, about 80% of active mutual fund managers have failed to earn the S&P "market" return, meaning they charged large fees but underperformed the benchmark they were hired to beat.

saving – the act of setting money aside for future expenses. You have to live on less than you make to be able to save.

sequence of returns risk – a significant downturn in the stock market when you first enter retirement. Over 100 years, the stock market return has been about 10%, but it can be much more volatile over shorter periods of time. Let's say Joe retired at the end of 2008 with a $500,000 portfolio. The market went down about 50% during the bear market 2007–2009. His portfolio would now be worth $250,000. That wasn't supposed to happen! It will take a 100% return on his $250,000 to get back to his original $500,000 portfolio. And it might take several years for his portfolio to get back to $500,000. Sequence of returns risk is one of the main reasons I recommend diversification.

sinking fund – money saved/set aside for a future expense (e.g., a vacation sinking fund). Sinking funds are typically funded by small amounts each month. If you know your vacation will cost $1,200, save $100 per month for twelve months; then you can go on a fully paid-for vacation.

Social Security – a tax, commonly called a payroll tax, and also a benefit. It's a government-run entitlement program. Beginning at age 62, if you have enough work credits, you are eligible to begin drawing Social Security income, which is a pension-like income stream that is designed to replace 30%–40% of your pre-retirement income—something of a safety net to help keep senior citizens out of poverty. Benefits are highly progressive, replacing more of your pre-retirement income if you're lower class and a smaller percentage for the middle and upper classes.

stock market – refers to the marketplace where you can buy and sell ownership stakes in publicly traded companies. It's really a market of stocks; there are over 10,000 publicly traded companies that sell ownership stakes (via certificates or shares). A company can raise capital/funding via stocks or bonds. If you purchase shares (i.e., stock) in a publicly traded company, you are then a shareholder. As the underlying company makes money, your stock is worth more. Stocks have historically traded at 15–20 times the annual earnings of a company—this is referred to as the P/E ratio (company's stock price divided by its annual earnings). In essence, you're counting on the company still being in business fifteen to twenty years from now.

term life insurance – a contract with a financial company (e.g., MetLife) where the insured (you) pay monthly premiums to get life insurance coverage over a set period of time (e.g., 20 years). The policy value is paid to the beneficiary (e.g., spouse or children) in the event of the insured person's death. Life insurance is meant to replace someone's income/salary to those that are dependent on this salary. A common suggested amount of coverage is ten times the insured's salary.

umbrella policy – paying premiums to an insurance company for secondary insurance coverage. You are purchasing additional coverage in the event of a large claim. This is additional insurance on top of your existing insurance, typically homeowners and car insurance. This can prove beneficial if you are involved in a car accident (that you caused) and multiple drivers sue you for damages. Most car insurance will have a relatively low payout per individual accident. In other words, your existing car insurance most likely has a maximum amount it will cover. After this maximum coverage amount is reached, you are on the hook for any additional liability. I recommend an umbrella policy once you hit your thirties or forties and have reached a modest net worth.

wants – expenses that are best categorized as desires. Examples include: country club dues, vacation, spa treatment, entertainment.

wealth – an abundance of money and/or possessions, sometimes used as a synonym for net worth.

whole life insurance (a.k.a. permanent) – a hybrid insurance product that is part term life insurance, part investment vehicle—expensive premiums compared to stand-alone term life insurance and typically has a low rate-of-return (compared to the S&P 500 index). It does have some tax advantages that might be beneficial to a very small portion of the population. It has a cash value that can be borrowed against.

zero-based budget – a monthly plan for how to spend your disposable income (take-home pay). The reason that it's zero-based is because you start each month from scratch and decide how to spend that month's income, rather than using last month's budget. Don't let the prior month's budget carry over and become this month's budget without using some critical thinking and evaluating your spending priorities each month. If you can't justify the expense, the default amount allocated to that category is zero.

REFERENCES

About the Author
Gillespie, Lane. "Bankrate's 2024 Annual Emergency Savings Report." Bankrate. June 20, 2024. https://www.bankrate.com/banking/savings/emergency-savings-report/#n3i.

Introduction
Reed, Eric. "Study Says 40% of Workers Forced Into Early Retirement: Here's How to Stay Ahead of the Curve." SmartAsset. July 19, 2023. https://smartasset.com/retirement/40-percent-americans-forced-to-retire.

Chapter 1
Batdorf, Emily. "Living Paycheck To Paycheck Statistics 2024." *Forbes Advisor*. April 2, 2024. https://www.forbes.com/advisor/banking/living-paycheck-to-paycheck-statistics-2024/.

Brock, Catherine. "How to Boost Your Retirement When Social Security Only Covers 40%." The Motley Fool. April 26, 2021. https://www.fool.com/retirement/2021/04/26/how-to-boost-your-retirement-when-social-security/?irclickid=3YEV4mQIFxyNTxFynYTiz1qwUkCUt1xZrzrcWk0&utm_campaign=mpid&utm_medium=affiliate&irgwc=1.

Cachero, Paulina. "Most U.S. College Grads Don't Work in the Field They Studied, Survey Finds." *Bloomberg*. 2022. https://www.bloomberg.com/news/articles/2022-04-18/is-college-worth-it-most-graduates-work-in-other-fields?embedded-checkout=true.

Kotsakis, Teddy. "Disability Facts." Plus Financial Network. September 12, 2023. https://www.pfnins.com/blog/disability-facts#:~:text=The%20odds%20of%20becoming%20disabled,22%20chance%20of%20becoming%20disabled.

Langone, Alix. "One Third of Workers Are Making A Big Mistake With Their 401(k)". *Money*. June 12, 2019. https://money.com/one-third-of-workers-are-making-a-big-mistake-with-their-401k/.

"Historical Average Stock Market Returns for S&P 500 (5-year to 150-year averages)." Posted by Cory Mitchell. TradeThatSwing. September 12, 2024. https://tradethatswing.com/average-historical-stock-market-returns-for-sp-500-5-year-up-to-150-year-averages/#:~:text=The%20average%20yearly%20return%20of,including%20dividends)%20is%207.454%25.

Renter, Elizabeth. "Most Americans Save, but Many Can't Cover a $1,000 Emergency." nerdwallet. May 9, 2023. https://www.nerdwallet.com/article/banking/data-2023-savings-report?trk_location=ssrp&trk_query=60%2525%2520of%2520americans%2520lack%2520a%2520retirement%2520specific%2520savings%2520account&trk_page=1&trk_position=0.

Turner, Terry. "49+ US Medical Bankruptcy Statistics for 2023." RetireGuide. October 20, 2023.

https://www.retireguide.com/retirement-planning/risks/medical-bankruptcy-statistics/.

U.S. Bureau of Labor Statistics. "Entrepreneurship and the U.S. Economy." 2016. https://www.bls.gov/bdm/entrepreneurship/entrepreneurship.htm.

Vanguard. "How America Saves." 2024 https://institutional.vanguard.com/insights-and-research/report/how-america-saves.html#research-report.

Walrack, Jessica. "Avoid Becoming One of These 6 Retirement Statistics." U.S. News & World Report. September 26, 2023. https://money.usnews.com/money/retirement/articles/avoid-becoming-one-of-these-retirement-statistics.

Chapter 2
Cruze, Rachel. *Love Your Life, Not Theirs*. Brentwood, TN: Ramsey Press, The Lampo Group, LLC., 2016.

Chapter 3
Principal. "Principal Financial Well-Being Index." 2016. https://www.principal.com/about-us/global-insights/well-being-index-insights.

Chapter 5
DeParle, Jason. "Record Rent Burdens Batter Low-Income Life." *The New York Times*. December 12, 2023. https://www.nytimes.com/2023/12/11/us/politics/rent-burdens-low-income-life.html.

Dougherty, Connor. "The Rent Revolution is Coming." *The New York Times*. October 15, 2022. https://www.nytimes.com/2022/10/15/business/economy/rent-tenant-activism.html.

Heeb, Gina. "The Math for Buying a Home No Longer Works." *The Wall Street Journal*. December 11, 2023. https://www.wsj.com/finance/home-ownership-mortgage-interest-rates-122a272f.

Chapter 6

Davis, Maggie. "Average Car Payment and Auto Loan Statistics: 2024." LendingTree. September 20, 2024. https://www.lendingtree.com/auto/debt-statistics/

Chapter 7

Beebe, Jeanette. "Lifetstyle Creep: What It Is and How It Works." *Investopedia.* Updated July 23, 2024. https://www.investopedia.com/terms/l/lifestyle-creep.asp.

Chapter 8

Gallo, Carmine. "70% of Your Employees Hate Their Jobs." *Forbes.* November 11, 2011. https://www.forbes.com/sites/carminegallo/2011/11/11/your-emotionally-disconnected-employees/.

Pippin, Sonja, Rixom, Brett, and Wong, Jeffrey. "Improving Critical Thinking Skills." *Strategic Finance.* November 01, 2021. https://www.sfmagazine.com/articles/2021/november/improving-critical-thinking-skills/.

Chapter 9

Hanson, Bo and Preston, Brian. "4 Financial risks that are worth taking!" *The Money Guy Show.* Podcast video, YouTube. November 10, 2023. https://www.youtube.com/@MoneyGuyShow/search?query=4%20financial%20risks%20that%20are%20worth%20taking.

Hanson, Bo and Preston, Brian. "Entrepreneurship vs Employment: Which Path Leads to Financial Success?" *The Money Guy Show.* Podcast video, YouTube. February 2, 2024. https://www.youtube.com/watch?v=TbWJfmgoqx4&t=1905s.

Chapter 10

GinsGlobal Index Funds. "94% of US Fund Managers underperform S&P 500 over 20 years." March 22, 2022. https://www.ginsglobal.com/articles/94-of-us-fund-managers-underperform-sp-500-over-20-years/.

Iacurci, Greg. "More retirement savers are borrowing from their 401(k) plan. Those are 'leading indicators of economic stress' expert says." CNBC. December 10, 2023. https://www.cnbc.com/2023/12/10/more-americans-take-401k-loans-an-indicator-of-financial-stress.html#:~:text=About%202.6%25%20of%20savers%2C%20or,2022%20and%201.7%25%20in%202020.

"Historical Average Stock Market Returns for S&P 500 (5-year to 150-year averages)." Posted by Cory Mitchell. TradeThatSwing. September 12, 2024. https://tradethatswing.com/average-historical-stock-market-returns-for-sp-500-5-year-up-to-150-year-averages/#:~:text=The%20average%20yearly%20return%20of,including%20dividends)%20is%207.454%25.

Putnam Investments. "Time, Not Timing, is the best way to capitalize on stock market gains. **S&P 500 Index, 12/31/07–12/31/22**." Cetera. https://www.myfinancialsense.com/time-not-timing.

Walrack, Jessica. "Avoid Becoming One of These 6 Retirement Statistics." U.S. News & World Report. September 26, 2023. https://money.usnews.com/money/retirement/articles/avoid-becoming-one-of-these-retirement-statistics.

Chapter 12

Backman, Maurie. "25% of Americans Expect No Social Security Benefits in Retirement." The Motley Fool. July 10, 2021. https://www.fool.com/retirement/2021/07/10/25-of-americans-expect-no-social-security-benefits/.

Congressional Budget Office. "CBO's 2022 Long-Term Projections for Social Security." December 16, 2022. https://www.cbo.gov/publication/58564.

Statista. "Number of retired workers receiving Social Security in the United States from 2010 to 2022." August 23, 2024. https://www.statista.com/statistics/194311/number-of-us-social-security-payments-received-by-retired-male-workers/.

Taylor, Kelley R. "Calculating Taxes on Social Security Benefits." Kiplinger. June 12, 2024. https://www.kiplinger.com/retirement/social-security/604321/taxes-on-social-security-benefits.

Chapter 13
Kiyosaki, Robert. *Rich Dad, Poor Dad.* Scottsdale, AZ: Plata Publishing, LLC., 2017.

Kline, Daniel B. "68% of Americans with debt doubt they will ever be debt-free." *USA Today.* January 11, 2018. https://www.usatoday.com/story/money/personalfinance/budget-and-spending/2018/01/11/68-of-americans-with-debt-doubt-they-will-ever-be-debt-free/109354554/.

Lemke, Tim. "8 Common Causes of Debt – and How to Avoid Them." WiseBread. 2024. https://www.wisebread.com/8-common-causes-of-debt-and-how-to-avoid-them.

Chapter 14
Jason & Patti. "6 Types of FIRE to Pursue – Financial Independence Retire Early." Our Life on Fire. December 20, 2020. https://ourlifeon-fire.com/types-of-fire-to-pursue-financial-independence-retire-early/.

Robin, Vicki. *Your Money or Your Life.* New York: Penguin Random House, LLC., 2018.

Chapter 15

Hanson, Bo and Preston, Brian. "Millionaires Share Their Secrets to Financial Success! (2023 Edition)." *The Money Guy Show*. Podcast video, YouTube. June 30, 2023. https://www.youtube.com/watch?v=_QpuAQaflIo.

Ramsey, Dave. *Baby Steps Millionaires*. Franklin, Tennessee: Ramsey Press, The Lampo Group, LLC, 2021.

Stanley, Thomas J. and Fallaw, Sarah Stanley. *The Next Millionaire Next Door*. Lanham, MD: Lyons Press, 2018.

Chapter 16

Orem, Tina and Parys, Sabrina. "Tax Planning: 7 Tax Strategies and Concepts to Know." nerdwallet. January 16, 2024. https://www.nerdwallet.com/article/taxes/tax-planning.

Chapter 17

Kilroy, Ashley. "8 Different Types of Insurance Policies and Coverage You Need." May 24, 2022. *Forbes* Advisor. https://www.forbes.com/advisor/insurance/types-of-insurance-policies/.

Silvestrini, Elaine. "How to Pay for Long-Term Care." Kiplinger. September 24, 2024. https://www.kiplinger.com/retirement/long-term-care/how-to-pay-for-long-term-care.

Vettese, Frederick. *The Essential Retirement Guide*. Hoboken, New Jersey: John Wiley & Sons, Inc., 2016.

Chapter 18

Brock, Fred. *Retire on Less Than You Think*. New York: Times Books, 2007.

Moss, Wes. "How Much Do You Need to Retire? (Less Than You'd Think)." *BiggerPockets Money*. Episode #492. Podcast video, YouTube. January 16, 2024. https://www.youtube.com/watch?v=HVMyZ7no2eI&t=2121s.

Reed, Eric. "Study Says 40% of Workers Forced Into Early Retirement: Here's How to Stay Ahead of the Curve." SmartAsset. July 19, 2023. https://smartasset.com/retirement/40-percent-americans-forced-to-retire.

Shenkman, Jonathan. "Are You Ready to Retire? Find Out With This 10-Item Checklist." Kiplinger. November 7, 2023. https://www.kiplinger.com/retirement/retirement-checklist-are-you-ready-to-retire.

Vettese, Frederick. *The Essential Retirement Guide*. Hoboken, New Jersey: John Wiley & Sons, Inc., 2016.

Chapter 19

Berger, Rob. "5 Alternatives to the 4% Retirement Withdrawal Rule." *Forbes*. October 1, 2023. https://www.forbes.com/sites/robert-berger/2023/10/01/5-alternatives-to-the-4-retirement-withdrawal-rule/.

Berger, Rob. "How To Understand Sequence of Returns Risk." *Forbes* Advisor. July 6, 2021. https://www.forbes.com/advisor/retirement/sequence-of-returns-risk/.

Chapter 20

Principal. "Principal Financial Well-Being Index." 2016. https://www.principal.com/about-us/global-insights/well-being-index-insights.

Schatz, Paul. "Why People Don't Participate in Their 401(k) plans . . . And Why That's a Big Mistake." Heritage Capital LLC. November 17, 2020. https://investfortomorrow.com/retirement-planning-2/why-people-dont-participate-in-their-401k-plans-and-why-thats-a-big-mistake/.

Chapter 21
Dayton, Howard. "2,350 Bible Verses on Money." 1973. https://encour.nl/wp-content/uploads/2015/08/2350-verses-on-money.pdf.

Chapter 22
Bradberry, Travis. "Ten Habits of Incredibly Happy People." December 10, 2021. *Forbes*. https://www.forbes.com/sites/travisbradberry/2017/02/14/ten-habits-of-incredibly-happy-people/.

Woolley, Suzanne. "How Much Money Do You Need to Be Wealthy in America?" May 15, 2018. Bloomberg. https://www.bloomberg.com/news/articles/2018-05-15/how-much-money-do-you-need-to-be-wealthy-in-america?embedded-checkout=true.

Chapter 23
Elkins, Kathleen. "1 in 6 Millennials Have $100,000 Saved – Here's How Much You Should Have at Every Age." CNBC Make It. February 5, 2018. https://www.cnbc.com/2018/02/05/1-in-6-millennials-have-100000-heres-how-much-you-should-have-saved.html.

Kasperkevic, Jana. " A Third of Millennials Share Their Salary Information With Co-Workers." Marketplace. October 18, 2017. https://www.marketplace.org/2017/10/18/millennials-sharing-salary-information-equal-pay/.

Makridis, Christos. "The American Dream Lives On, as 80% of Millennials Expect Same or Better Lifestyle Than Parents." *Forbes*. October 12, 2020. https://www.forbes.com/sites/christosmakridis/2020/10/12/nearly-80-of-millennials--gen-z-believe-they-will-be-same-or-better-than-parents-new-survey-finds/#:~:text=Topline%3A%20Amid%20rising%20inequality%20and,as%20good%20as%20their%20parents'.

McGrady, Vanessa. "Facebook Eavesdropped on Millennials to Learn Their Money Mindset." *Forbes*. February 2, 2016. https://www.forbes.com/sites/vanessamcgrady/2016/02/02/facebook/.

Morgan, Blake. "NOwnership, No Problem, Why Millennials Value Experiences Over Owning Things." *Forbes*. January 18, 2019. https://www.forbes.com/sites/blakemorgan/2019/01/02/nowner-ship-no-problem-an-updated-look-at-why-millennials-value-experi-ences-over-owning-things/.

Notte, Jason. "Of Course 2 out of 3 Millennials Don't Have Credit Cards." TheStreet. June 19, 2016. https://www.thestreet.com/personal-finance/of-course-2-out-of-3-millennials-don-t-have-credit-cards-13608756.

Walsh, Kristen. Newsroom. Bentley University. Market research from Bentley found that 66% of millennials want to start their own business. July 16, 2019. https://www.bentley.edu/news/millennial-entrepreneurs-advice-early-starter.

Chapter 28
Scoon, Nicola. "45 Hot Take Questions to Spark a Friendly Debate." Polly. Accessed December 1, 2024. https://www.polly.ai/blog/hot-takes#What-is-a-hot-take.

Chapter 29
Anderson, Nancy. "6 Easy Ways to Tell If You Are Good With Money." January 8, 2017. *Forbes*. https://www.forbes.com/sites/nancyander-son/2017/01/08/6-easy-ways-to-tell-if-you-are-good-with-money/.

Fidelity. "How much do I need to retire?" August 21, 2024. https://www.fidelity.com/viewpoints/retirement/how-much-do-i-need-to-retire.

Hanson, Bo and Preston, Brian. "5 Levels of Wealth and How to Achieve Them! (2024 Edition)." *The Money Guy Show.* Podcast video, YouTube. January 12, 2024. https://www.youtube.com/watch?v=7yN6pfJpBdk&t=63s.

Conclusion

Admired Leadership. "Good Leaders Help Others to Recognize Harmful Patterns in Their Behavior." April 11, 2024. https://admiredleadership.com/field-notes/good-leaders-help-others-to-recognize-harmful-patterns-in-their-behavior/.

ACKNOWLEDGMENTS

I'm grateful to many individuals who helped me in my book calling. I refer to this as a calling because I do not know where the passion came from to write this book. I believe it was from the Lord above. It was a journey that took months, years if you include the original blog posts from which came many a chapter.

I've never written a book before, and as you might imagine, it takes a great deal of time. It took perseverance and more than a little help from my friends (to get by). I did it my way. Frank would have been so proud. Well, not so much. It's more Dennis the Menace style.

First, let me acknowledge the many informal editors that provided feedback on various chapters. Lyndsey and Marcus were the first two (other than my lovely bride) to review my first couple of chapters. Their thoughtful insights and perspective led to adding an introduction to the book as well as a glossary. I confess the glossary took me a couple of weeks. It was kinda like going back in time to when I wasn't familiar with the many personal finance concepts and terms in this book. Lyndsey is a budding personal finance mutant, like myself, always on a quest to learn more. Marcus is something of a philosophical savant. It's almost as if he got a philosophy degree from a renowned university in the North Carolina mountains. Marcus: philosophy major, purveyor of biblical truth, the seeker of serenity! The one, the only, Sir Ulrich Von Liechtenstein! Ok, maybe I got a little carried away on that last bit . . .

THE MIDDLE-CLASS MILLIONAIRE

I also want to thank my two financially independent friends James and Jeffrey. They both asked insightful questions and made thought-provoking suggestions. I very much appreciate your kind donation of time to reading several chapters, including at least one that was very much in draft status. Having a little constructive criticism is a healthy part of the writing process.

I am very grateful to Rosina, a close friend, who used her valuable time to read and edit my manuscript. Your observations, suggestions, and edits make the book more professional.

I also want to thank my mentor and longtime friend Phyllis. Her conversations, insight, and life example are truly an inspiration. She practices what she preaches! I will forever be grateful.

I also want to acknowledge the many inspirations I received from podcasts, YouTube videos, and personal finance books I've read over the years. I mentioned some in the references as well as in chapter 27.

I'm saving my highest praise for Heather, my loving wife and reluctant editor in chief. She was my support through this long and arduous process. She was my rock and someone I constantly leaned on. She was my editor in chief for my blog and my book. This involved editing many nights after a hard day of being both a mother and an ophthalmic technician. She read many draft versions of most every chapter. She must have often thought of Ruth Bell Graham, who, when asked if she ever considered divorcing Billy Graham said, "Murder yes, but not divorce." Seriously, she is my constant companion and steadfast confidant. She was willing to read and make suggestions on my many chapter iterations. She doesn't even like to discuss, much less read, personal finance topics. She'd prefer to wait for the movie. Being married to a baseball-loving, Star Trek-watching nerd requires her to take up her cross daily . . .

ABOUT THE AUTHOR

F inancial decisions are all around us. We make them almost every day. I created this book to share my experiences in the hope that you might learn from my successes, as well as my failures. Life's hard. Do your research and learn from your mistakes; better yet, learn from others' mistakes and avoid money pitfalls altogether. Helping others through personal finance education is a core passion for me.

I am intrigued by how people approach financial decisions. Some of these decisions turn out well, and some, well, not so much . . . I'm convinced that most financial mistakes can be avoided. Having said that, we're all human and prone to making poor financial decisions. Let's take a journey together and find ways to think smarter about our daily decisions and how they impact our personal finances. I don't claim to have all the answers, but I hope this book will help educate folks about how we can use money strategies and insights as we think smarter together.

You can't get where you're going until you know where you're starting from. Personal finance is like a road trip—financial independence is the destination. How you get there is personal and different for each person.

The picture of a road heading straight for the mountains (financial freedom) is our ideal route, but the truth is quite different. It's invariably a long and winding road.

I know my personal finance journey has had many ups and downs. I'll bet dollars to doughnuts you can relate. Perseverance, patience, and intentionality are traits that have helped along my journey.

I started working when I was ten, as a newspaper carrier for the *Indianapolis Star*, in Russiaville, Indiana—small-town America. I used to get up at 3:30 a.m. Monday through Friday. This was something I chose to do to have some walking-around money. I didn't really understand finances, or how the world worked for that matter, but I knew it was a little easier if you had a few greenbacks in your pocket. I recall I made $64 a month. I learned early on that I had to be patient with customers who didn't always have the money when I came to collect each month. This was my first clue that some struggled with personal finances. I remember, on one occasion, having to deliver the papers in three feet of snow. I was hours late to most of the homes on my route, but there was satisfaction in completing the task at hand, and the customers were appreciative of my work ethic at such a young age.

I've had many jobs along my journey, including: janitor, lawn-care maintenance worker, leaf raker, snow shoveler, night crawler salesman, door-to-door book seller, vet clinic helper (a.k.a. pooper-scooper extraordinaire), parking attendant, tax accountant, auditor, analyst, staff accountant, accounting manager, and currently, financial planning and analysis manager.

I didn't have a passion for personal finance until, shortly out of college, I started reading *Debt Free Living* by Larry Burkett. I was fortunate enough to see him in person before he passed in 2003. He had a passion for helping people on their personal finance journeys. His book and presentation made a strong impression on me, especially his desire to help others with their financial struggles.

Around the age of 25, I began saving for my retirement. I started off small, saving around 10% of my salary (including company match) and ramped up to over 30% by my late forties. My average savings rate was 20% of my salary over the first twenty-five years of my career. My average income over those twenty-five years was about $100,000 per year. Saving early, while I was single, was a good first step, but I was about to enter the messy middle of my thirties.

Getting married, buying a house, starting a cabin rental business, having a special needs child, spending too much on a new car . . . are just a few of the twists and turns that led to my long and winding road. A long and winding road that has led me to aspire to become a member of the FIRE community—Financially Independent, Recreationally Employed.

I have put together a beginner's guide on how to get you started on your personal finance journey, whether you're in your twenties, thirties, forties, or beyond. You have to start somewhere—destination: financial independence. I want this book to be a map. How you get there is up to you, but maybe you can learn from my journey and avoid some of the mistakes I made along my path.

I've read more than twenty personal finance books and teach personal finance classes, including Dave Ramsey's Financial Peace University.

The Millionaire Next Door, by Thomas J. Stanley, is my favorite personal finance book, but I've learned something from each of the books I've read (even if I disagreed with some of their approaches).

I wrote this book to help folks get started on their own personal journey toward financial independence. Once you're financially independent, you'll have more options on how to be the best version of you, and the freedom to focus on the passions that get you out of bed each day. Being stressed out about your finances isn't a dream, it's a nightmare.

My wife and I built a 7-figure nest egg by age 50 (with zero inheritance), and I want to share the wisdom I've gathered along the way so you can achieve your personal financial independence.

Let's take this journey together!

MY BACKGROUND

I'm a Christ follower. This affects every aspect of my life, including personal finance. I truly believe that many will continue to struggle with their finances (about 60% of Americans can't come up with $1,000 for an emergency) until they get their priorities in line with the Bible. When I applied God's priorities to my finances, I finally realized God's peace in my life.

It is my belief that many people try to fill the God-sized hole in their heart with other things, such as money, alcohol, or even work. These are but poor substitutes (temporary high) for a real relationship with the God of the universe! The same God that created the earth, the stars, the galaxy, even you and me.

I recommend the book *The Case for Christ* by Lee Strobel. I also enjoyed the movie of the same name, based on the book. I am a big fan of bestselling author and financial expert Dave Ramsey and his quest to help people become, and stay, debt-free. I attended his Financial Peace University class and highly recommend it. I have a bachelor of science in business administration and a master of accounting degree from the University of North Carolina at Chapel Hill.

I'm also a certified public accountant. Let me back up and define what an accountant is. An accountant is someone who tells you about a problem you didn't know you had, in a way you don't understand ...

I like sports (Go Heels! Go Panthers! Go Braves!), visiting the North Carolina mountains, spending time with family and friends, listening to music, watching TV, and reading personal finance books. I'm always up for a spirited discussion on current events, personal finance, politics, business, technology, generational differences, and religion.

I'm a husband and father. My goal is to follow God's path on this winding road of life so my family is provided for spiritually and financially.